Crisis in the Life of an Actress

AND OTHER ESSAYS ON DRAMA

SØREN KIERKEGAARD

Crisis in the Life
of an Actress

AND OTHER ESSAYS ON DRAMA

*translated with an introduction
and notes by Stephen Crites*

HARPER TORCHBOOKS
Harper & Row, Publishers
New York and Evanston

First Edition: HARPER TORCHBOOKS, 1967
Harper & Row, Publishers, Incorporated,
New York and Evanston.

Library of Congress Catalog Card Number:
67-10676.

CONTENTS

TRANSLATOR'S PREFACE

Completing this modest translation has very much increased my respect for the patience and skill of my betters, the translators of Kierkegaard's major works into English. Their occasional murmurs of complaint about the difficulty of the task are not only justified but under the circumstances remarkably restrained. One can only salute the achievements of Lowrie, Dru, and the Swensons in bringing such delicate cargo to British and American shores over such perilous seas with so little loss. It is often said that Kierkegaard was both the best and worst of stylists. In either case the style is difficult to translate. At his best he is at once passionate and ironically detached, capable of prickly wit and sublime pathos, concrete yet subtle both dialectically and poetically. Sentences move with an uncanny balance through intricacies of thought and image, making surprising turns, setting several nuances to vibrating simultaneously, reaching for a witty touch here and a polemical slash there, yet never breaking stride. At his worst he is mannered, tortuous, and ambiguous. He has a fondness for converting adjectives into abstract nouns and for making technical terms of such cumbersome expressions as the one which I was obliged to translate as 'feminine youthfulness'. Whether at his best or worst – and both can appear within a single paragraph – he leaves many pitfalls for the translator who tries to duplicate the performance on a different terrain.

The translations which have followed those earlier, major ones seem to be marked by longer and longer introductions, at least in proportion to the length of the texts. Since I view this trend with some dismay I am embarrassed that my own introduction to this translation should be such a flagrant instance of it. Also I have to admit that the three essays translated can be understood without reading the introduction. They are self-contained. On the other hand some historical background may add a dimension. In particular, the actress who inspired the main essay is well worth getting acquainted with. Furthermore, the aesthetic theory in which the essays are grounded may be somewhat obscure to the modern reader, and is besides a neglected side of Kierkegaard's thought. This seemed a convenient place in which to discuss it, in relation to other aspects of his work. Finally, *The Crisis and a Crisis in the Life of an Actress* had a significance for Kierkegaard's own life and career as an author quite independent of the essay's own particular content. It played a strange role in a religious crisis in his life and came to have an important part in his final interpretation of his authorship as a whole. At any rate, discussing all these things required a disgracefully large portion of this thin volume, and that is the way outrages are committed: one thing leading to another.

I owe a great debt to my good friend Tharald Borgir who is a talented Norwegian musician, to August Albertsen who was at Wesleyan for a year as a Norwegian exchange student, and to the distinguished Danish physicist–philosopher Aage Petersen, each of whom compared portions of my translation, at some stage in its preparation, with the Danish original. It was my final good fortune that the translation came into the hands of Erik A. Langkjaer of Harper & Row, who subjected it to a last painstaking comparison with the original. His sensitive ear for both the Danish and English languages resulted in numerous corrections and valuable stylistic suggestions. I am also indebted to my Wesleyan faculty colleagues James Lusardi and Louis O. Mink for perceptive criticisms of the content and the English style of portions of the translation and introduction. Between them, all of these men have spared the reader many barbarities, obscurities, and plain mistakes. But I have been stubborn at some points, and bear the full blame for those that remain. I am also grateful to Miss Irene Parmelee for typing the final draft with unusual care, and to Wesleyan University for a summer research grant which enabled me to complete the translation.

INTRODUCTION

i. *Three Artists of the Theatre:*
Actress, Playwright, and Spectator

On 23 January 1847, The Royal Theatre in Copenhagen opened a new production of Shakespeare's *Romeo and Juliet*. The role of Juliet was being played by Johanne Luise Heiberg, then thirty-four years old and for many years a popular leading lady of the Danish stage. But playing Juliet held a special significance for her, because she had played the same role on that same stage almost twenty years earlier, as a girl not yet sixteen. Hanne Pätges, as she had then been called, was a child of German-born parents, hence foreigners in Denmark, and besides that quite poor in money and all too rich in children. So Hanne had experienced a good deal of hardship in her early years, alleviated only by her modest success as a dancer and child-actress. But her Juliet had scored a sensation, and had really launched her career. Yet she did not return to the role until 1847, as a mature artist. Søren Kierkegaard was in the audience during a performance of this later production, and was deeply impressed by her Juliet. He had admired her artistry for many years, but in addition had been preoccupied with the diverse modes of the category of 'repetition'. The artistic triumph of Fru Heiberg's return to the role in which she had made her name as a young girl eventually elicited from him a brief work to which he gave the long title, *The Crisis and a Crisis in the Life of an Actress*.

Fru Heiberg herself took the opportunity to comment some years later on these two portrayals of Juliet, and also on Kierkegaard's little study, in a large scale autobiography written during the latter part of her life. This fascinating autobiography was published in two thick volumes some years

after her death under the title, *A Life Relived in Recollection*.[1]
Her own reflections on her two appearances in the great love-
tragedy show a remarkable consonance with Kierkegaard's; so
much so that one suspects that her recollection has been influenced by his interpretation. She had played the role the first
time, she says,

> like a child who sings a charming song without knowing the
> notes. I felt a childish joy in expressing the lovely thoughts
> and surrendered myself to them, never dreaming of the
> difficulties of the role. I was borne along by my fantasy, my
> feeling. People found in my acting what was perhaps really
> there, but I was unconscious of it and could have given no
> account of it. Nielsen, who played Romeo, said that he was
> very delighted to play opposite his young Juliet.[2]

The public and the critics were as enthusiastic as her leading
man. But even at the time, she had been embarrassed when
the newspaper critics praised her for the reflectiveness which
they thought she had brought to the role, and in retrospect she
was convinced that no sixteen-year-old girl could really grasp
the demands of this role. At best, a young girl might comprehend the early scenes in the play, when Juliet appears as a
child of fourteen. But even then,

> one must not forget that she is a fourteen-year-old girl in
> the south and not in the north. But in the fourth act she
> appears as a fully-developed woman, powerful, energetic,
> who does not even shrink from the most terrible things,
> from that which would even make a man tremble. She
> knows what she wants, and she works her will with courage,
> with a courage which does not shrink even from the gates
> of death. A very young girl can therefore play the first part
> of the role perfectly well, but never the last, the most

---

[1] *Et Liv gjenoplevet i Erindringen* (København: Gyldendalske Boghandel, 2nd ed., 1904).
[2] *Et Liv*, I, p. 57. Translations from this work are mine.

important part of the task. An actress can perform the first part by means of *art*, so that an illusion can be created, but the young girl cannot produce the effect of the fully developed woman by means of art, because this requires maturity in artistic development, a real artist possessing virtually everything that time, experience, and cultivation can bring. All the nuances of a woman in love are present here, the whole scale, from the first immediate surrender to the height of the demonic passion.[3]

When she undertook the role again almost twenty years later, Fru Heiberg did set out to capture all these nuances, bringing all her training as an actress and her experience as a woman to the task. She wandered along the harbour until late at night rehearsing her lines and working herself into their poetry and into the pathos of the dramatic situation. The role became such an obsession that this pious woman became fearful that she was involving herself in an act of idolatry.

But this later production, in 1847, was not a popular success. Michael Wiehe, who played Romeo, had created quite a sensation two years earlier when he played the role opposite a sixteen-year-old girl, but his collaboration with Fru Heiberg was ill-fated. There was a conflict in styles between the two principals, the opening-night performance was interrupted by cries of 'Fire!' (which turned out to be a false alarm), and there were other obstacles. Disappointed, the actress soon turned to other roles.

Between her two appearances as Juliet, Fru Heiberg had not only gone from triumph to triumph as an actress, but had come to preside over the most celebrated salon in Copenhagen. She enjoyed this position, not only because of her own talent and charm, but also because she was the wife of Denmark's leading man of letters, Johan Ludvig Heiberg. Like

[3] Ibid., I, p. 416.

many other savants of that time, Heiberg was a man of astonishing versatility. His greatest achievements were as a poet and playwright, but he also had a considerable influence on Scandinavian culture as a literary critic. Furthermore, he wrote philosophical works, was the editor of a succession of journals, experimented and wrote treatises in astronomy, and was a substantial force in Danish social and political life. Heiberg had spent several years in France and Germany in the 1820s, and so was in a position to bring the great intellectual forces of Europe to bear on the then somewhat provincial cultural life of Denmark. He was impressed with late romantic literature, and was interested in the possibilities of French vaudeville (a farcical and rather fragmented form of musical comedy). At the same time, he was deepening his own Scandinavian roots. He lectured for a time in Danish language and literature at the University of Kiel, and wrote on Danish language and Nordic mythology. According to his wife, he did not find Germany congenial to his 'Danish nature'. As he later declared in a poem: 'To die in Copenhagen is better than to live in Kiel.'[4]

Yet at Kiel Heiberg came under the influence of Hegelian philosophy, which he was to have an important part in introducing into Denmark. Hegel was then the reigning monarch of philosophical thought in northern Germany, and in 1824 the young Dane propelled himself enthusiastically into the master's intellectual orbit, reading his works and becoming personally acquainted with Hegel and his leading disciples in Berlin. However, as he reported in his *Autobiographical Fragments* with typical dramatic flair, he did not really get to the heart of the Hegelian System until he was sitting one day in his room in the Hotel König von England in Hamburg, 'with Hegel on my table and Hegel in my thoughts' and with chorales sounding in the background from the bell-tower of St.

4 Quoted in *Et Liv*, I, p. 33.

Petri-Kirche, when suddenly 'like a flash of lightning' that illuminates a whole landscape in an instant, he understood and was convinced; the experience gave him 'a peace, a security, a self-consciousness, that I had never known before.'[5] Heiberg was not the only Dane to receive the Hegelian philosophy ecstatically, as a kind of revelation. Søren Kierkegaard was to exploit the comic possibilities of this phenomenon with fine irony. But it was no joke to Heiberg, who had promptly injected a treatise on human freedom into a philosophical debate concerning freedom and determinism then current in Copenhagen, and proudly claimed afterwards that this had been the first Danish treatise written from the Hegelian standpoint, a standpoint which was to dominate Danish thought during the next few decades. Not only did Heiberg continue writing philosophical works from a somewhat modified Hegelian standpoint, but he also credited the Hegelian philosophy with having liberated him for his vocation as a dramatic poet. Hegel's Absolute is neither an ideal domain separated from concrete existence, nor is it the whole of existence regarded as an undifferentiated unity. It inheres precisely in the concrete particulars, and is progressively realized in the apparent rough-and-tumble of particular events, primarily in human history. Its own inner dialectic is fully realized only in the total process of development through progressively higher states of consciousness, but it is present, implicitly, in every form of human consciousness. By revealing to him the positive relation of the finite to the infinite, Hegel had refined Heiber's strong pantheistic bent to the extent that he could take seriously the limited, finite, and even farcical

---

[5] This experience is discussed, with some treatment of Heiberg's influence on Kierkegaard, in Rohde, Peter P., *Sören Kierkegaard in Selbstzeugnissen und Bilddokumenten* (Hamburg: Rowohlt Taschenbuch Verlag, 1959), pp. 18–22. See Kierkegaard's parody in *Concluding Unscientific Postscript*, tr. Swenson & Lowrie (Princeton University Press, 1941 and Oxford University Press, 1942), pp. 163–167.

aspects of existence, so much so that he could devote himself to the creation of a Danish vaudeville, along with other theatrical ventures.

Heiberg returned to Copenhagen in 1825, won success as a dramatic poet, especially in a comic vein, and a few years later wooed and won the enchanting young leading lady of the Royal Theatre. Hanne was eighteen years old when they were married in 1831, her already-distinguished groom being twenty-one years her senior. Not only did this alliance occupy a brilliant place in the artistic and social life of Copenhagen, but as a marriage it seems also to have been a genuine love-match, at least as it is recalled in Fru Heiberg's memoirs. However, this well-favoured marriage created a minor crisis in protocol for the Royal Theatre: should the young actress henceforth be referred to as Madame Heiberg or as Fru (Mrs.) Heiberg? It was customary to apply the 'Madame' to married actresses, but Heiberg was a titular professor, and the Danes like most Europeans were acutely sensitive to matters of rank. Would not the distinction of her husband, and hence her own station, be better reflected by use of 'Fru'? But that suggestion 'aroused much chatter in little Copenhagen'.[6] Since the authorities could not decide, this delicate matter of decorum was finally referred to His Majesty King Frederik VI. By royal decree 'Fru Heiberg' henceforth appeared on the playbill. In the years that followed she appeared in many of her husband's plays and vaudevilles, often in roles created especially with her in mind, and also in many of the plays which he translated for the Danish theatre from the French. The psychologically complex heroines of late romanticism were her special forte. So their stars continued to ascend together in the compact firmament of Danish cultural life, and they gathered the other leading cultural lights around them in their salon. By

[6] *Et Liv*, I, p. 143

the 1840s Heiberg was virtually the reigning cultural authority of Denmark.

Also in the 1840s a body of literature began to appear in Copenhagen which was quite different from Heiberg's and often quite polemical against it. Although these works appeared with astonishing rapidity and were mostly pseudonymous, they were generally recognized to be the work of a single author, and those at all familiar with the small circle of Danish literateurs recognized through these diverse personae the voice of Søren Kierkegaard. Except for the first, *Either/ Or*, however, these works did not even approach being 'best sellers' – even on the modest scale which 'best sellers' would have to assume in a language spoken by only about three million people. His works were frequently difficult to understand, and his highly original technique of 'indirect communication' succeeded in being so indirect that virtually no one could detect the thread of continuity running through them. Certainly Heiberg, who read a good many of Kierkegaard's works, had no very clear idea what he was trying to do. But the anti-Hegelian polemic in Kierkegaard's writings became increasingly clear and sharp, and Heiberg could hardly have found this very congenial. Heiberg himself was also the target for many sly jibes, mostly put forth rather light-heartedly though sometimes also with a heavy hand. Kierkegaard launched a number of these drolleries in his little book of *Prefaces*, written under the pseudonym 'Nicolaus Notabene'. In a 'Preface' to a proposed new philosophical journal, obviously a parody of some of Heiberg's editorial efforts, Nicolaus proposes to make the riches of philosophy available in simple enough terms that every man, including even perhaps himself, will be able to understand; hence the journal may be able to synthesize intellectual and commercial interests, unlike most philosophical journals, by turning a profit. As for poor Nicolaus himself, his best hope is that his failure to understand philosophy may be *aufgehoben* in a marvellous new Hegelian synthesis:

I am so stupid that I cannot understand philosophy; the antithesis of this is that philosophy is so clever that it cannot comprehend my stupidity. These antitheses are mediated in a higher unity: in our common stupidity.[7]

At the same time, again with Heiberg's philosophical efforts in view, Nicolaus declares that one of the many things he cannot understand about philosophy is how a work can have 'gone beyond Hegel), as it seems to suggest in the closing paragraphs, when the work appears to him to have done nothing but parrot Hegel throughout.[8] Kierkegaard seized every opporunity to poke fun at the Danish epigones who were 'going beyond Hegel'; the phrase became a kind of refrain in some of his works.

Heiberg especially excited Kierkegaard's sense of the comic by putting together a gilt-edged, highly ornamented book called *Urania: Yearbook for 1844*, published, as he himself announced, as 'a New Year's gift especially for the aesthetically cultivated public'. This elegant book contained a 'Star-Calendar for 1844' and an article on 'The Astronomical Year' by Heiberg, along with miscellaneous essays by himself and others. There are many oblique jokes about this book in Kierkegaard's works, including his reference to 'a decorative copybook, very dainty and elegantly put together, with many

---

[7] *Forord. Morskabslaesning for enkelte Staender efter Tid og Leilighed*, af Nicolaus Notabene (Kjøbenhavn, 1844), Ch. VIII, Sec. 3.

[8] In his journal *Perseus*, Heiberg published a good deal of his own work, including an article on 'The Logical System', in which he remarked that Hegel's logical construction had been subject to 'imperfections in details', and concluded by saying that it was obvious 'how much the presentation offered here differs from the Hegelian' (*Perseus* No. 2, pp. 5, 44). In a review of *Perseus* No. 1 the philosopher Sibbern declared that Heiberg was beginning 'to go beyond Hegel' (*Maaneds skrift for Litteratur*, XIX, 1838, p. 292).

blank pages' in *The Crisis* (p. 82 below). Nicolaus Notabene naturally devotes one of his 'Prefaces' to *Urania*. He is willing to leave to the specialists the question whether 'the Herr Professor's recent astronomical, astrological, chiromantical, necromantical, horoscopical, metoscopical, chronological studies will really be a gift to science and mankind . . .' His own anxiety has been 'that Prof. H., who has always been a philosopher as well, should suddenly undergo a new metamorphosis and step forth as the one who has come to earth to solve the riddles of theology'. On behalf of theology he is therefore relieved that Heiberg's interest in the celestial has directed him instead to astronomy.[9] Some rancour lay behind all this wit, because one of Heiberg's contributions to *Urania* was a review of Kierkegaard's *Repetition*, which Heiberg meant to be friendly but which quite missed the point and then offered a rather patronizing Hegelian correction of what Heiberg took the point to be. Kierkegaard wrote a lengthy retort which is really a most illuminating explanation, in philosophical terms, of his alternative to Hegelian 'mediation'. But he never published it, except in a shortened version as a footnote to *The Concept of Dread*. [10]

However, Kierkegaard was a great admirer of Heiberg's plays, and his works contain many allusions to them. He remained personally on generally friendly terms with the

[9] *Forord*, IV.
[10] *The Concept of Dread*, translated with an Introduction and Notes by Walter Lowrie (Princeton University Press, 1946 and Oxford University Press, 1944), pp. 16–17n. Lowrie discusses the dispute and quotes a large portion of Kierkegaard's valuable but unpublished retort in his introduction to *Repetition* (Princeton University Press and Oxford University Press, 1946). Apparently *Prefaces* originated in a plan to write a full-scale polemic to be called 'New Year's Gift by Nicolaus Notabene, published for the benefit of the asylums'. Probably the little joke in *Prefaces* about Professor Heiberg's turning to astronomy rather than theology is an oblique reference to the fact that Heiberg, in his review, misconstrued Kierkegaard's category of repetition as a natural, rather than religious category.

Heibergs. In his earlier years he frequented their salon and contributed various youthful pieces to Heiberg's journals. He registered his enthusiasm for a novel by Heiberg's mother, Fru Gyllembourg, in a small book entitled *A Literary Review*, which used the novel as point of departure for a sharp critique of 'the present age'.[11] Then his high regard for Fru Heiberg, as an actress and as a woman, is implicit in *The Crisis*. He even resolved that if *The Crisis* were ever published in book form it should be dedicated to 'Hr. Prof. J. L. Heiberg' as 'Denmark's Aesthetician', by his own pseudonym as a 'subaltern aesthetician'. He adds in the same journal entry:

God knows I have always meant well by Heiberg, since I always hold fast to my first impression. But he has not behaved properly toward me. Yet even after that time [presumably the Corsair crisis] I have done what I could to hold him essentially in honour.[12]

As it was, *The Crisis* first appeared in a supplement to the newspaper, *The Fatherland*, in four instalment, 24–27 July, 1848. It was published under the pseudonym *'Inter et Inter'*. If the pseudonym kept anyone in doubt about the identity of the author, at least Fru Heiberg was fairly sure, and although she is not named in the work she recognized that she and her art were its subject. In 1851 Kierkegaard acknowledged that the piece was his in a little pamphlet 'On my Work as an Author', which he sent to Fru Heiberg along with a copy of *The Crisis*. He included a little note with the following dedication:

---

[11] The latter part of *A Literary Review* has been translated by Alexander Dru under the title *The Present Age*, recently reissued in Fontana Library of Theology and Philosophy and Harper Torchbooks.

[12] *Søren Kierkegaards Papirer*, udgivne af P. A. Heiberg og V. Kuhr, Vol. IX, A (Kjøbenhavn: Gyldendalske Boghandel, 1920), IX, 187. (References to the *Papirer* are cited by entry number, not page.) This passage is not translated in Dru's edition of the *Journals*.

To

the lucky artist,

whose sensibility and will-power have even been

– again how lucky! – just as great as her luck,

Fru Heiberg

with admiration

from the author.

Kierkegaard explains in the note that he does not wish to impose on her to read the pamphlet on his work as an author, but he does want her to know, as the pamphlet explains, that he had been the author of *The Crisis*. If she had not chanced to notice the article when it appeared in *The Fatherland* he hopes that she might find 'an idle hour which could be filled by reading it'. For

to speak frankly, the little article is directed particularly to you. Whether in its time it was read by many or by few – if you have not read it, then according to the author's view it has not achieved its purpose. On the other hand, if you have read it – and if you have found it to be in felicitous even if not perfect accord with your own thoughts on the subject: then according to the author's view it has entirely achieved its purpose.[13]

As a matter of fact, Fru Heiberg had been delighted and flattered by the article, and in her autobiography expressed surprise that an author who was not himself an actor could

[13] Heiberg published this note and dedication in his preface to the work when he reissued it in 1856. This edition, with Heiberg's preface and notes, was incorporated in *Søren Kierkegaards Samlede Vaerker*, udgivne af A. B. Drachmann, J. L. Heiberg og H. O. Lange (Kjøben-havn/Kristiania, Gyldendalske Boghandel, Nordisk Forlag, 1904), x Bind. The note and dedication are found on p. 322, Vol. x, and in the notes to Vol. 14 of the new edition (Gyldendal, 1963), p. 210, and are also quoted by Fru Heiberg in *Et Liv*, 1, pp. 424–25. The reference to the actress's luck recalls the passage translated p. 73 below.

exhibit such keen psychological insight into the life of the theatre, and could find words for what she had felt but could not express. Her husband appears to have been pleased as well. Only a little over a month after Kierkegaard's death in November 1855, Heiberg reissued the article, along with Kierkegaard's dedication and note to Fru Heiberg. He supplied some explanatory footnotes, of which I have made use in my notes to the translation, and contributed a short paragraph explaining the circumstances under which the essay had been written, adding that it

well deserves to be read anew, if for nothing else for the contempt with which it disposes of the utterly incompetent theatre critic in all his aesthetic poverty and moral depravity.[14]

Heiberg had been the Director of the Royal Theatre since 1848, and his régime was a stormy one, rather unhappy for both himself and his wife. When he republished Kierkegaard's essay only a few months before his resignation, he had ample reason to wish to see the newspaper critics soundly castigated again. Heilberg also edited and reissued other works of Kierkegaard's; the fact that *Prefaces* was among them is evidence of his good humour and magnanimity.

Heiberg died in 1860. His wife retired officially from the Royal Theatre in 1858, largely in protest against the new management of the theatre, but she appeared occasionally for several years thereafter, making 'farewell appearances' in the manner of the great ladies of the stage. She took her final bow as an actress in 1864. As a stage director from 1867–74 she was a protagonist of progressive movements in the theatre, and was influential in getting Ibsen's plays produced in Denmark; he showed his gratitude in some warm verses dedicated to her. She died in 1890. Her unusual book of memoirs, published

[14] *Søren Kierkegaards Samlede Vaerker*, x, p. 321.

some years later, reveals a remarkably fresh and thoroughly feminine personality whose theatrical sensibilities are alive even in her writing, in her control over many different moods, and her sense for the detail which manifests the dramatic even in commonplace events. In these pages one meets a woman and an artist well deserving of the homage paid her by the author who had been so impressed by her portrayal of Juliet.

ii. *The Aesthetic and the Existential*

I have implied that Kierkegaard's talents as a 'spectator' were such as to entitle him to a place alongside the Heibergs as an 'artist of the theatre'. I shall present some of the evidence for this rather large claim in the next section, devoted largely to Kierkegaard's writings on drama. He was certainly not a conventional drama critic. Drama was the art-form which he knew best and to which he felt most akin, but his observations were informed by a general theory of art which exhibits the intricate dialectical reflection he brought to all his work. Furthermore, his relatively neglected aesthetics has an important dialectical relation to other and better-known aspects of this thinking. Before turning to his interpretation of art we will explore this relationship. The aim in these two sections is to provide some context in Kierkegaard's thought as a whole for the works translated here.

Kierkegaard's general aesthetics is left largely implicit in his writings. He never attempted to produce a complete systematic theory of art, but for reasons which had nothing to do with his well-known polemic against 'the System'. His primary task as a writer lay elsewhere, and besides he seems to have considered that the basic groundwork of aesthetic theory had already been laid. Kierkegaard was, broadly speaking, a Hegelian in aesthetic theory. Certainly many of his aesthetic views were highly original; his own genius burned too brightly for him to be a mere epigone or imitator. But for the basic theoretical background which informed his aesthetic thinking he drew heavily on Heiberg and other Hegelian writers, and even more on Hegel's own *Aesthetik,* to which Heiberg's work had introduced him. This debt will be fairly evident to anyone acquainted with Hegelian aesthetics when we discuss Kierkegaard's writings on art in the next section. Kierkegaard was speaking for himself when he declared through his pseudonym in the first volume of *Either/Or* that the field of aesthetics had found its master in Hegel.[15]

It is worth asking why Kierkegaard, who is quite properly regarded as the great anti-Hegelian of the nineteenth century, should have been such an unabashed Hegelian in his aesthetics. To be sure, Hegelian ideas and expressions turn up in Kierkegaard's writings even when his basic intent is most anti-Hegelian; but in aesthetics he acknowledges Hegel as the master. It is possible for the Hegelian philosophy to be supreme as an interpreter of art, yet necessarily wrong-headed in treating ethics and religion, so Kierkegaard thought, because this philosophy is itself 'aesthetic' in the broadest sense. Not, of course, that Hegel's philosophy is simply art-theory. 'The aesthetic' in this broader sense, otherwise identified by Kierkegaard as 'the aesthetic-speculative' or 'the aesthetic-metaphysical' (in *The Crisis,* p. 90 below), is a very inclusive category which embraces science and philosophy as well as art, and can also be adopted as the basis for a whole way of life. Kierkegaard of course distinguishes 'aesthetics' in the narrower, purely artistic sense, from this inclusive category, but in order to grasp his view of the former it is

---

[15] Doubleday Anchor edition, p. 51. It can never be taken for granted that the pseudonyms express Kierkegaard's own views, but in this case there is no reason to doubt it. There are many appreciative references to Hegel in this volume, and the influence of Hegel is apparent throughout Kierkegaard's aesthetic writings.

necessary to explore the broader category under which it is subsumed.

'The aesthetic' in its most comprehensive sense, is derived from the Greek verb αἰσθάνομαι, which means literally 'perceive', 'apprehend by the senses', 'learn', 'understand', 'observer'. As William Barrett points out, both 'theatre' and 'theory' have the same Greek root as 'aesthetic'.

At a theatre we view spectacles in which we ourselves are not involved. The spectacle may be either interesting or boring, and the 'interesting' and the 'boring' are the dominant categories under which the aesthete views all experience. The intellectual who looks at things with detachment, the philosopher who claims to be the spectator of all time and existence – both are fundamentally aesthetes in their attitudes.[16]

Broad as it is, the category of the aesthetic signifies a particular standpoint towards reality, the standpoint of objective apprehension. Every man adopts this category in so far as he becomes a knower or a subject of experience. Reality is received in the mode of more or less formed and therefore comprehensible objects of experience, and is valued to the extent that this objectification issues in forms which are internally coherent and can also be understood in relation to one another. A person is, in this mode, essentially an observer, the subject to whom the objects become manifest. That the experiencing subject also participates in existence, and hence suffers its contingencies and its limitations of perspective, is accidental and irrelevant, is in fact precisely the aspect of his situation which he must try to overcome in the aesthetic relation.

---

[16] Barrett, W., *Irrational Man: A Study in Existential Philosophy* (Doubleday Anchor edition, 1962; cf. Heinemann edition, 1961), p. 164.

The category of the aesthetic is essentially timeless, since the goal of this process of objectification is the transmuting of reality into a system of internally related ideal forms. Of course these forms must in some manner inhere in existing reality, but existing reality is of aesthetic interest only in so far as the ideal forms emerge in it, perhaps in the course of a perpetual cycle or in a process of development such that the idea implicit at the outset becomes progressively more explicit, i.e. develops from potentiality to actuality. In any case time is reduced to the accidental. This is a point of great importance to Kierkegaard. Time is an ineradicable feature of existence itself. It can be neither halted nor reversed. Therefore the decisions that are required of every existing individual are momentous and irrevocable; even though they are never made with the security of complete knowledge, a man is bound to their consequences. But there are no such risks in the aesthetic sphere, in which the individual abstracts himself from his situation in existence to enjoy the pure play of ideal possibilities, for which existence only furnishes the medium. For example, in Hermann Hesse's *Steppenwolf*, the existential impasse of the beaten and melancholy hero is overcome in a magic theatre, in which he is able to participate in such a way that the limitations of existence, of time in particular, are negated. He exchanges witty profundities with Goethe and Mozart, who of course dwell in the pure aesthetic heaven of the magic theatre; he relives his old, unhappy loves in such a way that they now turn out well; he murders his current love, but it is understood that the 'pretty picture-world' of the magic theatre is not afflicted by anything so irreversible as death, so that although he has been guilty of bad form the hero will be able to perform the scene again, hopefully with happier results. Kierkegaard would surely have applauded this conception of the magic theatre as a fine poetic representation of the aesthetic itself.

Of course, apprehension or experience has many modes, and

the ideal forms are embodied in diverse media. The arts have made use of lines, shapes, colours, sounds, verbal images, etc., but the purpose is to take a medium, so to speak, out of existence so far as possible, so that it can be transparent to or subservient to the idea. We shall return to this problem. It should be noted, however, that in Kierkegaard's view all science also takes up the aesthetic stance, since it attempts to organize experience of the existing world into pure conceptual forms for the purpose of gaining objective knowledge. But philosophy, as Hegel argued, is the ultimate medium for the idea, since thought is the idea's own pure element; so philosophy is able to grasp in pure ideality what art had first expressed in a material medium, and what a natural science could grasp only for a limited purpose and within a limited frame of reference. This does not mean that speculative philosophy could simply replace art or science. A particular idea cannot come to expression at all apart from its appropriate medium, and it can never come to satisfy 'the whole man' in the austere medium of pure thought with the same intensity as in the sensuous media of art. But Hegel tried to show that philosophy can grasp ideas, once given, in their purity and in their necessary relation to one another as logical moments in the absolute Idea. To Kierkegaard this meant at least that it is possible to approach art philosophically, and at most that speculative philosophy might justly claim to be the supreme intellectual realization of the aesthetic standpoint in general.

The difficulty in Kierkegaard's eyes is that a pretentious philosophy, or a science or art form which refuses to accept its limits, may attempt to collapse all human relationship to existence into the aesthetic category. In fact, although there has been much dispute among philosophers about the way men experience or know, and even about the possibility of knowledge, most philosophers have taken it for granted that men's only encounter with existence, or the only one worth mentioning, is in the subject–object relationship, that is, in experience. It has been generally recognized that man is a creature of feeling and emotion as well as perception and knowledge, but these are all modes of the aesthetic. What Kierkegaard calls the aesthetic has been implicitly regarded as so all-embracing, particularly since Descartes, that it has not been recognized as a distinct category at all. Kant, in distinguishing practical or moral from theoretical reason, was an exception to this tendency among philosophers; but Hegel carried it to its fruition in the System, as the standpoint of absolute Subject. Kierkegaard, on the other hand, insisted that experience, knowledge, feeling, apprehension, do not exhaust the possibilities of human encounter with existence. Men do not merely apprehend existence. They are in existence. They are not only the subjects of experience but potential agents of act and decision. Kierkegaard therefore undertook to define the limits of the aesthetic–speculative standpoint, and to set another standpoint over against it, the existential, which he explored and evoked throughout much of his work as a writer. This distinction between the aesthetic and the existential was drawn with particular clarity and detail in *Either/Or* II and *Concluding Unscientific Postscript*, but it is at least implicit in all his major works.

Kierkegaard drew the distinction with great passion as well as precision, because its implications were close to his heart. He insisted that the existential spheres, the ethical and the religious, are fundamentally misconceived when they are subsumed under the aesthetic category. To exist ethically, for example, is to accept the limitations of temporal existence, is to make decisions in full consciousness that they are irreversible and that they will condition the future for good or ill. The ethical man is also concerned with the universal, not, however, as an object to be apprehended in abstraction from the conditions of existence, but as an ideal which it is his duty to bring into existence by his resolute act. (The influence of Kant is evident in Kierkegaard's view of the ethical life.) It is of course possible to assume a position 'beyond good and evil' provided we take up our stand on the mountain-top, in the thin, clear air of the aesthetic. The intrusion of ideas of good and evil into the study of history or sociology is an inhibition to the essential task of comprehension, and is usually parochial in its motivation; likewise, the intrusion of such ideas into art can only violate its integrity as art. The fact that people are motivated by ideas of good and evil may have to be reported by the social scientist and represented by the artist; an Iago may even be deliberately exhibited by the artist as a figure of evil. But the purpose is to experience, to comprehend, not to pass ethical judgement. The ethical indifference of the aesthetic category, however, does not signify that good and evil are transcended in its 'magic theatre', but only that a particular standpoint has been adopted, the standpoint of the observer rather than that of the agent. Since the observer as such is essentially timeless, he can possess and enjoy contradictory possibilities in the mode of reflection which could not coexist as realities in time. Good and evil are therefore not relevant to the observer as such, since he is not called to decision; they are relevant to the man of whom a resolute act is required, under the conditions of existence in which a man must do either one thing or another, and cannot have it both ways. Furthermore, in the religious in its most eminent sense, in Christianity, the existing individual has a new problem: that he is a sinner whose powers are set in active rebellion against God, and therefore cannot redeem himself through exercise of these same active powers. Even the ethical cannot acknowledge this problem because the ethical is confounded by it, and the aesthetic can scarcely so much as suspect the existence of such a problem. Moreover, the individual is obliged to decide about his relation to an intrinsically paradoxical claim: that a historical individual, Jesus of Nazareth, is his God and Saviour. Faced with this stupendous claim, his own limitation as a finite individual is accentuated to the utmost, since his reason cannot resolve this paradox, yet his decision will determine his present existence and future destiny. In fact, such a decision can be made only by the grace of this same God and Saviour.

Now, if one makes the ethical or the religious into a matter for objective consideration in the media of art, science, or philosophy, he must consider them from the observer's position, which is outside the existential situation in which actual ethical or religious decisions must be made. Such a procedure is like using a camera to capture a lion. Having a good picture is not the same as struggling with the lion, even though the picture may be valuable in itself, and useful in preparing for future encounters with lions. There are of course cognitive elements in any decision; one must have some knowledge of what one is deciding about, the clearer the better, and for Kierkegaard there is even a knowledge which 'edifies', which makes a man aware of his situation and clarifies for him the nature and implications of the decision which he faces. But there is no knowledge available to an existing individual from which a real decision could simply follow, as a logical conclusion from secure premisses. Hegel's attempt, however, to absorb ethics and religion into a comprehensive system of objective knowledge, by making the ethical or religious consciousness itself into an objectified datum, simply obscures the leap of decision and thereby confuses the categories. The existential standpoint is simply collapsed into the aesthetic category, the 'either/or' decision faced by the individual existing in time is vaporized into the 'both/and' of ideal possibilities envisaged by an essentially timeless observer. Hence Kierkegaard's 'unsystematic' ('unscientific') polemic against Hegel, and hence also his tortuous quest for an appropriate way to address himself to the existential. For it seemed to him that a systematic critique, and also a direct and systematic exposition of his position, would have to be developed in terms of the aesthetic category over which Hegel held sway, and hence could be transmuted into merely another paragraph in the System.

He was as concerned as Hegel himself that the method employed should be the reflex of the content, but in Kierkegaard's case the 'content' was existential, a way of life founded on decision, to be evoked rather than described, and therefore not a 'content' at all in the ordinary sense. In opposition, therefore, to Hegel's beautifully self-reflexive System of objective thought, Kierkegaard sought to develop a self-reflexive style of existential communication modelled on Socratic midwifery. But Socrates, of course, was not a writer. Kierkegaard's most serious methodological problem was how to communicate evocatively, socratically, indirectly, as a writer. As we shall see in the two final sections of this introduction, Kierkegaard drew heavily, with perhaps an excess of ingenuity, upon the arts of the theatre in his attempt to solve this methodological problem. Much art was required – in order to elude the aesthetic.

Kierkegaard's preoccupation with the distinction between the aesthetic and the existential was not aroused simply by what seemed to him to be the confusion of the categories which had resulted from philosophical imperialism, however. In fact, he saw the attempt to accommodate existence to the standpoint of the philosophical spectator as simply a grandiose projection of a way of life prevalent in the modern world. There has been much discussion of Kierkegaard's conception of the aesthetic way of life, and we need not linger over it here. Abstractly considered, it is the attempt to live exclusively in the aesthetic category, as the collector of interesting experiences. The 'aesthetic man' may attempt to transmute all existence into art or science, or his objectification of life can take crasser forms. In either case he abdicates his own authentic existence as an 'individual', and at the extreme can sink into the 'perdition' of a Johannes the Seducer, a connoisseur of ingeniously contrived erotic adventures but incapable of the 'decision' of love, and hence so lost to genuine existence that it is as though 'his feet were so formed that he left no footprints.'[17]

Kierkegaard's pseudonymous works are devoted chiefly to illuminating the existential, particularly the problem of 'becoming a Christian' as the existential problem *par excellence*, against the backdrop of the aesthetic. In the earlier works the existential is set over against the aesthetic as a way of life; in the *Fragments* and especially the *Postscript* it is set over against the aesthetic in its philosophical projection as the System. The *Postscript*, as he later explains,

> having appropriated the whole pseudonymous, aesthetic work as the description of *one* way a person may take to become a Christian (viz *away* from the aesthetical in order to become a Christian), . . . undertakes to describe the other way (viz away from the System, from speculation, etc., in order to become a Christian).[18]

iii. *Kierkegaard as an Aesthetician*

If an aesthetic treatment of ethics and religion must necessarily and fundamentally distort the ethical and religious life, it is nevertheless obvious that no such problem exists for an aesthetic treatment of art. It is entirely appropriate, Kierkegaard thought, to approach art as a timeless observer, since one's aesthetic satisfaction consists precisely in being brought into relation to pure ideas through an appropriate medium. These ideas, of course, inhere in real life in the real world, though usually in a somewhat confused, mixed, or distorted

---

[17] *Either/Or*, I, p. 303.
[18] *The Point of View*, translated by Walter Lowrie (Oxford University Press, 1939), p. 42. The subjects treated in this section accordingly receive their fullest exposition in the *Concluding Unscientific Postscript*.

form. Hence the artist must be a sensitive observer of the world in order to construct the pure aesthetic models, and the spectator by contemplating these models can gain genuine insight into reality.

An 'idea' which finds expression in art does not have the purely intellectual connotation which the term is likely to have for a modern reader. It is not as though an artist contemplated a pure idea, then addressed himself to the technical problem of finding an appropriate medium for its expression. The idea comes to consciousness only in the process of artistic creation itself, and only in the appropriate medium. The problem in art, as Hegel had shown, is to shape the material or medium in such a way that it will become as transparent as possible to its proper idea, so that the idea can, as it were, shine through the medium employed. Kierkegaard was not concerned, as Hegel was, to show that all ideas are moments of greater or lesser adequacy in the absolute Idea, but he was persuaded that each medium is limited in the range of ideas that can be expressed in it. In fact, he believed that only a single idea could be perfectly embodied in a particular medium. For example, in his essay on 'The Immediate Stages of the Erotic' in *Either/Or*, I, he tries at some length to show that the idea of the immediate or sensuous erotic finds its ideal embodiment in music.

In the erotic-sensuous genius, music has its absolute object. It is not of course intended to say by this that music cannot also express other things, but this is its proper object. In the same way the art of sculpture is also capable of producing much else than human beauty, and yet this is its absolute object; painting can express much else than the beauty which is celestially glorified, and yet this is its absolute object. In this respect it is important to be able to see the essential idea in each art, and not to permit oneself to be disturbed by what it is incidentally capable of representing. . . .

The idea in language is thought, and we must not permit ourselves to be disturbed by the opinion of certain sentimental people, that its highest significance is to produce inarticulate sounds.[19]

It will follow that a truly classic work of art appears when a particular medium is formed in such a way that it contains its idea in perfect transparency. In the same essay, Kierkegaard undertakes to show that music had thus attained its classic form in Mozart's *Don Juan*; and since the immediate or sensuous erotic is such an elementally simple idea, in contrast for example to the rich complexity of reflection, Kierkegaard even goes so far as to suggest that this idea can receive only one absolutely classic expression, which of course turns out to be Mozart's master opera.[20] A further consequence of this view is that a particular idea can only very imperfectly be expressed in another medium. As illustration, Kierkegaard points to the alleged failure of all attempts, for example by Molière and Byron, to render the immediate eroticism of Don Juan in the medium of language. 'Language involves reflection, and cannot, therefore, express the immediate.'[21] On the other hand, language alone is able to express the diabolically reflective eroticism of Kierkegaard's own creation, Johannes the Seducer, whom Kierkegaard sets in quite conscious juxaposition to Don Juan in *Either/Or*, I.

As we have noted, Kierkegaard never elaborated his aesthetics in a single major opus. Instead he wrote a number of separate essays, each more or less self-contained. His method in each of these essays was to take up one particular aesthetic idea, and attempt to express its essential character in relation to its appropriate artistic medium or in relation to a

[19] *Either/Or*, I, p. 63.
[20] Ibid., pp. 52ff.
[21] Ibid., p. 68.

particular work of art or artist in which it is successfully embodied. There is usually a strong psychological interest in
these essays, since he attempts to indicate the personal conditions necessary in the artist for achieving his idea, or in the
observer for appropriating it correctly.

Kierkegaard's keenest interest as an aesthetician was in
drama, and most of the aesthetic essays and fragments treat
characters and situations whose acquaintance he had made in
the countless hours – surely among the most pleasurable of his
life – that he spent in the theatre. The only essays on drama
which are quite comparable in scope with *The Crisis* are those
which appear in the first volume of *Either/Or*: pre-eminent is
his treatment of 'the immediate erotic' in Mozart's *Don Juan*,
to which we have already referred. There is also an exploration
of the situation of betrayed love as a dialectical problem in
relation to three heroines of dramatic literature, and a poetic-
dialectical investigation of the idea of 'first love' with reference
to Scribe's play of that name; and there is an essay, in rather
Hegelian style, on the condition for the construction of tragedy
in the modern mode in contrast to the classical Greek, including a sketch, with veiled autobiographical overtones, towards
the development of a modern Antigone. Other treatments of
drama in the major works are fairly incidental, subordinated to
other concerns, yet of intrinsic interest. In *Repetition*, Con-
stantine Constantius treats us to a memorable excursus on the
essential nature of farce, in the course of which he describes
two gifted farceurs of the stage of the Königstädter Theatre in
Berlin, Beckmann and Grobecker. Beckmann in particular is
praised for his ability to 'come walking' on the stage in such
a way that he projects a whole village environment, with a
crowd of street-urchins trooping at his heels. 'Indeed Herr
Beckmann is a pure economy for a theatre, for when it possesses him it has no need of street-urchins or painted scenery.'[22]

[22] *Repetition*, p. 57.

Madame Nielsen, Fru Heiberg's friendly rival on the Danish stage, receives her due in a long footnote to the 'Observations about Marriage' attributed to Judge William, Kierkegaard's spokesman for the ethical life in *Stages on Life's Way*.[23] Her particular genuis is again referred to in the closing pages of *The Crisis*, where Kierkegaard alludes to the footnote in *Stages*.

The Crisis officially brought Kierkegaard's strictly aesthetic writings to a close. He had in fact written very little in this area for some years. *The Fatherland* had carried an article in two parts in its issues of 19–20 May, 1845, on Mozart's *Don Juan*, provoked by a new production in Copenhagen of this opera which he so dearly loved, and constituting something of a postscript to his great essay in *Either/Or* (the article was attributed to the same pseudonym). *A Literary Review*, on the novel by Heiberg's mother, was published in 1846, but was more concerned with social criticism than aesthetics. Yet this dwindling of his aesthetic works did not stem from any loss of interest in aesthetic subjects, or in the theatre. His religious discourses were now simply demanding virtually all his energies as a writer. Aesthetic sketches do, however, continue to appear in his unpublished papers. For example, in 1847 he prepared an outline for a piece on his old friend, the actor C. N. Rosenkilde, in the role of Hammer in Heiberg's *The Inseparables*. And even after he had so resolutely decided to close his aesthetic writings with the publication of *The Crisis*, he wrote the article entitled 'Herr Phister as Captain Scipio'. It was completed in December 1848, under the pseudonym *Procul*. He intended at least to give a copy of it to Phister, who was a neighbour of his, and a long-time favourite as an actor. Apparently he also considered the possibility of letting it be published in *The Fatherland*. In a comment attached to

---

[23] Translated by Walter Lowrie (Princeton University Press, and Oxford University Press, 1940), pp. 133–34n. See pp. 137–138 below.

the article, he directs, however, that if it is published a note should be included explaining that the author 'was not very eager to have it published, because it was written in great haste and has not been revised'. In point of fact it had been rather carefully corrected, but Kierkegaard's intention was apparently that the article should be published in such a way that, in a sense, it would not count. Actually he left it unpublished, but for reasons that probably had nothing to do with the intrinsic worth of the article.

The article on Phister and the postscript on *Don Juan* are included in this translation, along with *The Crisis*. Although these three essays are written on a modest scale, and certainly belong among Kierkegaard's minor works, they are good examples of his method and style as an aesthetician. *The Crisis* in particular is a little gem of Kierkegaardian aesthetics, in which he undertakes to exhibit the modes in which the idea of 'feminine youthfulness' is embodied in the genius of a particular actress. The expression of this idea would seem to be so bound to a limited period in the actress's life that it would be particularly vulnerable to the erosions of time, but a central argument of the piece is that such is not the case. The genius that expresses this idea enjoys the same invulnerability to time as is conferred by any other essential relation to idea, for this idea, like others, is achieved by art. When she herself is quite young, in fact, the idea of feminine youthfulness can only be expressed in her in an unconscious way, with only a potentiality for the fully transparent expression. But Kierkegaard's primary interest is the 'crisis' in which this gestating idea is born into the clear light of conscious art, her 'metamorphosis' into full maturity as an artist. Kierkegaard brings a good deal of psychological insight to bear on the personal factors involved in this metamorphosis, and in discussing the obstacles to its completion is able to fire a few salvos in his ongoing polemic against 'the present age'. But the fundamental intent is to explore the nature of the metamorphosis itself, the immanent development from the potential presence of the idea to its full manifestation. This immanent development is of great importance to Kierkegaard's view of the aesthetic; it is, as he suggests (p. 90 below), a kind of paradigm of the aesthetic–metaphysical dialectic itself. Nothing radically new is brought to pass. Rather, the metamorphosis unfolds as 'a more and more intensive return to its first condition', all in essential relation to a single idea. This strictly aesthetic metamorphosis is contrasted in the article with one of a more ethical interest, but still an immanent development, in which over a period of years another actress (Madame Nielsen is the model) is able to express to perfection the whole succession of stages in a woman's life. But the really decisive contrast is not mentioned in this article, since it is beyond aesthetic comprehension altogether: this is the religious category of repetition, in which a man 'receives himself back again' by being reconstituted as a new creation through a transcendent act of divine grace. The aesthetic metamorphosis of our actress is obviously not a 'repetition' in this sense, since it does not require a transcendent act of re-action. Yet in her art she is unscathed by time; Fru Heiberg could be called a darling of the gods in the Greek sense, since as an artist she has been made for ever young.

In the sketch of Phister, Kierkegaard turns to the idea of reflective comedy, showing how the actor exhibits this particular genius in making a stock role in a commonplace comedy into a rare work of comic art. The little piece on Zerlina's duet with Don Juan returns to the theme of his great essay on Mozart's opera in *Either/Or*: the idea of the immediate erotic, with some further suggestions regarding the realization of this idea in the approach of the singers to their roles.

In all these articles, the polarity between immediacy and reflection is basic. The actress of *The Crisis*, for example, moves from an immediate to a more reflective relation to her

idea. In the reflective mode everything is brought into the
clarity of conscious thought, is deliberately contrived by the
artist and can be exhaustively understood by a perceptive
observer. This mode is explained most clearly in the article on
Phister. Phister is said to be so clear about every move he
makes that the critic who also has a gift for reflection – and
Kierkegaard's own genius was certainly of the reflective sort –
is able to achieve a complete consonance of understanding
with the artist himself. The immediate, on the other hand, is
uncontrived and intuitively expressed, a mode of art as unconscious as the song of a lark. The spectator can only sense its
power and respond to its beauty. For example, when the
actress of *The Crisis* expresses the idea of 'feminine youthfulness' in her early 'immediate' phase, as a young woman herself, the aesthetician can only wonder at her, but cannot
understand her or 'define' what she 'possesses' (though Kierkegaard does in fact go pretty far towards such a 'definition').
But the hero of the immediate is Don Juan, whose eroticism is
frequently referred to as a force of nature, guileless, direct,
and overpowering. The characters in the opera, including even
the particular figure of Don Juan himself, are not so much
consciously self-determined individuals as satellites whirled
about in the magnetic field of Juan's sheer erotic power, which
is expressed in the music.[24]

It is important to note that individuality is always an
accidental feature of the aesthetic, a feature which can be sup-
pressed either at the pole of pure reflection, where mind
merges with mind in the ideality of thought, or at the pole of
immediacy, which lacks clear contours of differentiation.
Hence the freedom from time enjoyed in the aesthetic. The

---

[24] This polarity between immediacy and reflection in Kierkegaard's
aesthetics is paralleled in an interesting way by the polarity between
the Dionysian and the Apollonian in Nietzsche's *The Birth of Tragedy*.
Of course there is no direct influence, and the two polarities do not
exactly correspond.

basic reason why the individual is never essential in the aesthetic is that the aesthetic does not concern itself essentially with decision, by which 'the individual' in the eminent sense is both presupposed and constituted (i.e. Kierkegaard's 'individual' comes to be precisely in the act of decision). By contrast, 'the individual' is the keystone of the existential, is in particular, Kierkegaard declares, 'the category through which, in a religious respect, this age, all history, the human race as a whole, must pass.'[25]

Yet Kierkegaard insisted that the aesthetic, beyond the ravages of times and the arduousness of individuality, carries its own legitimate and quite autonomous satisfaction. Art, in particular, is not to be justified by its contributions to purposes extrinsic to itself. Human consciousness is elevated by its participation in art, and this elevation is in itself of priceless value. According to Kierkegaard's aristocratic view it is also rare, since its attainment requires not only severe discipline but an attitude of receptivity and independence of mind to which few people even aspire. Even in his treatment of aesthetics Kierkegaard tends to stress the difficulties and the severity of discipline rather than the joy of the attainment, and the satisfactions themselves are made to seem rather austere. Yet he does clearly suggest that art is something in which to rejoice, and he certainly took an intense joy in it himself. Art, and any other intense experience or reflection, has the effect of sharpening sensibilities and deepening one's comprehension of the heights and depths, the order and the complexity, the menace, the beauty, and the wonder of the world of experience. It may deepen one's sense of the pathos as well as the joy of the world, but in either case the effect is profoundly humanizing.

[25] 'Two Notes about the Individual', published in English with *The Point of View*, p. 130.

iv. *The Role of the Aesthetic in the Religious Life and in a Christian 'Authorship'*

There are certainly many questionable features in Kierkegaard's treatment of art. So far as the details of interpretation are concerned, his writings speak for themselves, and the reader must decide for himself whether they shed any light on the subject or not. Beyond the details, the modern reader is likely to be doubtful about the idealistic premisses that inform his discussions of art, and may be troubled by the apparent separation of art from life, or at least from the ethical and religious centre of human existence. Since Kierkegaard rejects the speculative–idealistic interpretations of ethics and religion, but himself employs an idealistic interpretaton of art, art must necessarily be set on the opposite shore from the existential categories separated by the great gulf of his most decisive 'either/or'. Certainly the distinction between aesthetic and existential categories in Kierkegaard's dialectic does not seem to him to imply their total separation in life, as we shall see. But there remain serious problems, with which, in fact, a sympathetic critique of Kierkegaard might fruitfully begin.

The aim of this introduction is neither to criticize nor to defend, but if possible to shed some light on the works translated. I do think it is appropriate here to consider Kierkegaard's view of the role of art in the religious life, even though his essays on drama have nothing intrinsically to do with the subject. The three essays are written entirely from within the aesthetic standpoint; the religious lies beyond their horizon. But the two spheres were not so nearly separated in the life of the writer. As we shall see in the next section, Kierkegaard's decision to publish *The Crisis* was involved in a profound religious crisis of his own life, a crisis which brought to a head precisely the issue of his engagement, as a Christian author, in aesthetics. Furthermore, he engaged throughout his career in a remarkable kind of theatrics in fulfilling his very vocation as a Christian author. His preoccupation with drama was by no means peripheral to his own Christian task, however sharply he distinguished art from faith.

Let us examine the distinction more closely. It should be evident that Kierkegaard did not hold a low opinion of art, any more than he was inclined to belittle reflection.[26] Even the

---

[26] It is common enough, to be sure, to hear him accused of advocating sheer irrationality. He did oppose speculative rationalism as an all-embracing philosophical position, but he did not therefore propose irrationalism as the alternative. He did oppose prudential calculation and 'cleverness' as a sufficient guide to life, but he did not suggest that life ought to be lived, ethically or religiously, without the guidance of rigorous thought. He did attack a 'reflective age' because it lacked passion, and insisted that reflection could neither provide a sufficient substitute for the passionate decision to act nor in itself, without passion, provide a sufficient springboard for the decision to act. Yet he never suggested that decisions ought to be made without reflection; on the contrary, the more a man reflects the more capable he is of significant decision. Kierkegaard's own authorship is devoted to stimulating the kind of reflection that will make authentic decision possible (though, of course, not inevitable), and one of his central points is that no man can really make the decision of faith without understanding its implications.

Kierkegaard nowhere spells out more clearly his attack against passionless and therefore decisionless reflection than he does in *The Present Age*. Yet he is careful to add that 'just as reflection itself is not evil, so a very reflective age has its lighter side, simply because a higher degree of reflection implies greater significance than immediate passion; for when enthusiasm intervenes to gather the powers of reflection together into a decision, and because reflection confers, on the average, a greater capacity for action – then, when religion enters in, it takes command of that increased capacity for action.

'Reflection is not the evil; but a reflective condition and the deadlock which it involves, by transforming the capacity for action into a means of escape from action, is both corrupt and dangerous, and leads in the end to a retrograde movement.' (Translated by Alexander Dru, Fontana Library, Harper Torchbooks, 1962, pp. 67–68. See also pp. 84f.)

It is remarkable that in his introduction to the Harper Torchbook edition of this work Walter Kaufmann can still repeat the same charge he makes elsewhere, and on the basis of the same two quotations taken out of context from *Fear and Trembling*: that Kierkegaard depreciates

ethical man or the man of faith who has most resolutely rejected the aesthetic category as determinative of his life will
nevertheless find reflection indispensable and will find in art a
well-spring of refreshment and insight. It is even possible to
be an aesthetician or an artist – or scientist or philosopher,
presumably – yet live decisively in one of the existential
categories. Such a man will differ from the out-and-out
aesthete not by the fact that the aesthetic will be renounced,
but by the fact that it will be 'dethroned'. Judge William,
Kierkegaard's pseudonymous spokesman for the ethical life

reflection and thinks that passion should be substituted for it. (See
pp. 25–26. See also Kaufmann's *Existentialism from Dostoevsky to
Sartre*, Meridian Books, 1956, and Thames and Hudson, 1957, pp.
17–18: 'The crucial difference between an informed and uninformed,
a reasoned and un-reasoned, a responsible and irresponsible decision,
escapes Kierkegaard.' '. . . Kierkegaard rashly renounced clear and
distinct thinking altogether.' 'Reason alone, to be sure, cannot solve
some of life's most central problems. Does it follow that passion
can, or that reason ought to be abandoned altogether?' See also
Kaufmann's *From Shakespeare to Existentialism*, Doubleday Anchor
Books, 1960, pp. 195–96; Cf. Faber edition, 1960.) Even on its face,
it clearly does not follow from one of the quotations which Kaufmann
always cites – 'What our age lacks is not reflection but passion' – that
reflection should be diminished or abandoned. Although Kaufmann's
interpretation does seem to fit the other quotation – 'The conclusions
of passion are the only reliable ones, that is, the only convincing
conclusion' – it does not in fact. (The two quotations are from the
Doubleday Anchor edition of *Fear and Trembling*, pp. 53n, 109.) The
last clause, which Kaufmann omits two times out of three, already
suggests what Kierkegaard meant, and the contex makes it quite clear.
However much reflection may have preceded it, the 'conclusion' the
weight of which will be felt in existence and which will show what
a man has actually 'concluded' is the decision to act in a particular
way. But unless passion is brought to bear there can be no act. It does
not follow that passion is a substitute for reflection. Kierkegaard did
not endorse decisions based on a flip of a coin or on consultation of
the glands, and did not need to be told that 'millions may lose their
lives fighting for beliefs so utterly unfounded and inhuman that not
even such a bloody sacrifice can hallow them' (Kaufmann's Introduction to *The Present Age*, p. 26). One may sympathize with Kaufmann's
insistence that the bite, indeed the offence, of Kierkegaard's either/or
should not be mitigated. But it ought to be identified correctly; it is
not reason v. passion.

who speaks of this dethronement of the aesthetic in the ethical,[27] even argues that there are genuinely aesthetic satisfactions which cannot be enjoyed in the aesthetic life as such, but emerge only as a by-product of the ethical life; for example, the aesthetic satisfactions of marital love, which is an ethical relationship. In this respect the aesthetic is a 'lower' sphere of life than the ethical or the religious: The existential categories can absorb the aesthetic, but the aesthetic cannot absorb them. The ethical and the religious can be grasped in the aesthetic only in a distorted, essentially non-ethical or non-religious way, but the aesthetic can form an element in the ethical or religious life without being itself distorted or disintegrated.[28] The aesthetic still retains its autonomy. The aesthetic satisfactions stemming from the ethical life really are aesthetic. Similarly with the aesthetic possibilities of religion. Indeed, explicitly religious art created a serious problem for Kierkegaard, since he insisted that however religious its initial motivations might be it could succeed 'only in establishing an aesthetic relation to something aesthetic'.[29] He generally took the position that the Christian categories in particular simply do not mix with the categories of art, but there is no reason why the Christian individual cannot create and appreciate art in an aesthetic way.

For example, he argues in *The Works of Love* that the poet's task is in itself essentially non-Christian. But he cer-

[27] *Either/Or*, II, p. 230.
[28] It appears to me that Kierkegaard intends a similar asymmetry between the ethical and the religious, though it does not concern us in detail here. That the ethical is 'dethroned' in the religious is indicated by the fact that it may in an extraordinary case be 'suspended' by the higher claim. Yet it is not abrogated. When Abraham consents to sacrifice Isaac, it is not because he has risen to a new ethical standpoint, according to which the murder of sons is permissible, nor is the ethical set aside; the continued pressure of the ethical claim in face of the 'higher claim' is what creates the 'fear and trembling'.
[29] *Concluding Unscientific Postscript*, pp. 347–48.

tainly does not support any puritanical renunciation of poetry.
A Christian can be a poet and can enjoy poetry.

> A man would not be able to live every moment exclusively
> in the highest Christian ideal any more than he could live
> on the food from the Lord's table.[30]

Is all poetry, then, like unconsecrated food, nourishing but
profane? In general it is. Kierkegaard does make a distinction,
though it is not made as clearly as one would like. He admits
that 'there are also godly poets', whose 'songs are to the glory
of God, songs of faith and hope and love'. But a godly poet is
subjected to special difficulties, since such things must primarily be enacted rather than sung:

> . . . with invisible letters behind every word in Holy
> Scriptures a disturbing notice confronts him – for there it
> reads: go and do likewise. Does this sound like an artistic
> challenge, inviting him to sing?[31]

Kierkegaard offered no general prescription for resolving this
dilemma. Yet he himself was, if not precisely a godly poet, at
any rate a Christian author who, as he emphasizes in *The
Point of View*, had devoted his whole authorship to the service
of Christianity. He had certainly been aware throughout this
task of the 'invisible letters' commanding him to go and do
likewise, but he had attempted to 'sing' in such a way that the
song itself became a kind of act. It is of course impossible to
generalize from Kierkegaard's own case just what legitimate
use he thought an aesthetic work might have in the service of
the Gospel, but it is at least instructive to observe how he
himself set about being a Christian author.

[30] *The Works of Love*, translated by Howard and Edna Hong (Harper
& Row, and Collins, 1962), p. 61.
[31] Ibid., p. 60.

Kierkegaard saw himself as a poet as well as a dialectician, and had himself in mind when he wrote in his journal that being a poet

means having one's personal life, one's reality, in quite different categories from those of one's poetic work, it means being related to the ideal in imagination only, so that one's own personal life is more or less a satire on poetry and on oneself.[32]

In his pseudonymous writings he preserved a sharp distinction between his own person and the point of view of each particular work. When he wrote on art, as in the pieces translated here, he did so exclusively on aesthetic premisses. But he regarded his whole body of pseudonymous literature, from *Either/Or* through the *Concluding Unscientific Postscript*, as aesthetic in the broad sense, poetic and/or philosophical, yet the design of this whole body of work was to serve Christianity by exhibiting various alternative ways of life in such a way that the distinctive character of the Christian life could be brought to light. In such works as *Repetition, Fear and Trembling*, and *Stages on Life's Way*, for example, a person making the leap into the decisively religious is only described from the outside, by a pseudonymous narrator who merely glimpses the person as he disappears into a dimension of existence that the narrator cannot understand. In *The Concept of Dread*, the decisively religious is again just beyond the horizon, this time not a person making the 'leap', but the Christian category of sin, while the book restricts its treatment to the psychological category of dread which points towards sin. Kierkegaard did attempt quite directly to elucidate the Christian categories in the *Philosophical Fragments* and

[32] *The Journals of Søren Kierkegaard*, a selection edited and translated by Alexander Dru (Oxford University Press, 1938), 861. (Numbers refer to entries, not pages.)

Concluding Unscientific Postscript, but still in an aesthetic way, from a standpoint outside Christian faith itself. Johannes Climacus, Kierkegaard's pseudonym in these two works, makes it clear that he himself is not a Christian, at least not yet. Furthermore, in the *Fragments* Johannes claims only to be conducting a 'thought–experiment', spinning out a poetic idea: an idea to end all ideas, the idea of Absolute Paradox, which is being explicitly differentiated from the whole realm of aesthetic and ethical ideas. That the Absolute Paradox is really expressing the Christian categories is only indicated in a whimsical way, by having an objector spring to his feet at the end of each chapter and accuse the author of plagiarism. As we have noted (p. 28 above), the *Postscript* is the capstone of the pseudonymous literature, in which Kierkegaard speaks more directly about Christianity, and differentiates it from the philosophical System which is the speculative Summa of the aesthetic.

As we have also remarked in passing (p. 27 above), Kierkegaard employed a great deal of art in this ambitious attempt to point beyond the aesthetic. In particular, he drew heavily upon the arts of the theatre. It was no accident that he was on good personal terms with various actors and others connected with the Royal Theatre, since he himself had such a deep kinship to the craft of the actor or director or playwright. There is the same keenness of psychological observation, the sense of dramatic development and appropriate dramatic form, the ability to adapt his style to widely divergent *personae*. He does not simply define in general the various ways of life which are set forth as alternatives to the Christian, but exhibits them concretely from within, projecting himself dramatically into their roles. The poetically brilliant and tormented young aesthete whom we meet in the first volume of *Either/Or* writes no more like the benign Judge William of the second volume than Hamlet speaks like Polonius, and the 'seducer' whose diary concludes the first volume has a style

that distinguishes him from them both. His total pseudonymous production unfolds as a series of integrated theatrical
productions, a 'marionette theatre' as it has been called. One
has to go back to Plato to find a writer who employed anything
like so much dramatic art in essentially philosophical works.
Moreover, like an actor he calculated every gesture. He was
intensely concerned with matters which for most authors are
quite incidental to the publication of a work, such as the
appearance of the title-page. His own name did not appear at
all in most of the pseudonymous works, because he wanted it to
be clear that he personally was no more to be identified with
the point of view developed there than an actor is with the
character whom he portrays. If his name did appear, as editor
for example, it was to indicate a special relation between his
own position and that being expressed; e.g. on the title page
of the *Postscript* beneath the 'author', Johannes Climacus,
there appears the notation, 'Responsible for Publication: S.
Kierkegaard', because the *Postscript* is quite explicitly about
Christianity though it is not written from an expressly
Christian position. Again, the order and date of publication
were matters of great importance. Kierkegaard often with-
held a completed work until he thought the conditions had
been created for its proper reception, or arranged that the
publication date of certain works should coincide in order to
express a relation between them which would otherwise be easy
to overlook (and generally was overlooked anyway).

Kierkegaard did not limit this theatrical ingenuity to the
arrangement of his writings, however, since he intended that
his public life should be an extension of his authorship. He
was quite self-consciously on the stage in the impression which
he made in person, for the mystique of his 'indirect communication' required that he should appear to the public eye
in a guise which he regarded as necessary for the reception of
his works in a dialectically correct manner. He wished, for
example, to exercise a kind of Socratic midwifery through his

works. He addressed himself to basic issues involved in the
decisions each man must make regarding his way of life, but
he did not attempt to decide the matter for the reader. He did
not attempt to overpower the reader by argument or psychological manipulation, nor did he attempt to force a result on
him. Above all, he did not wish the reader to take his word for
anything. The works were to help the reader clarify the issues
for himself by the exhibition of the presuppositions, life-styles,
implications, and interaction of divergent ideas. Kierkegaard
attempted to withdraw personally from the works, so that a
reader could be left in peace to concern himself with the
problem of a book, leaving its author out of account. So
Kierkegaard not only employed the device of pseudonymity,
but cultivated what we should now call his 'image' as a 'draw-
ing-room hero,'[33] and appeared daily on the streets of Copenhagen as a gay, chattering man about town, not to be taken
personally as a serious thinker at all. And when the time came
for him to drop the trappings of pseudonymity, he fired the
first shot in a war with a satirical journal called *The Corsair*,
which ended by his being made a laughing-stock. It is doubtful
that he had actually anticipated just how far *The Corsair*
would carrying its campaign of ridicule, slander, and caricature, but even though he was deeply wounded he was prepared
to accept the attack as a blessing in disguise.[34] Now he could
get on with his serious religious works, in his own name, since
a point of great importance to him had been established by the
episode: that these works were 'without authority'. Though he
continues to emphasize this point in the prefaces, explaining
that the works were intended as aids to the reader's own self-
examination, it was the light in which he had been cast by the
Corsair episode which really made it possible for him to maintain the essentially Socratic relationship to his readers even on

[33] Ibid., 793.
[34] See Ibid., 588.

the solemn question of how to become a Christian. Works written under the name of one popularly regarded as an eccentric fool would have to carry their own weight, and the basic responsibility for the use made of them would be left to the reader himself. At the same time, because he had been able to break through the usual relationship between an author and his public, he considered that his writing had become a personal act. Indeed, as his pseudonym Johannes Climacus explains in *Philosophical Fragments,* the Socratic relationship is the highest possible between man and man, just because each is left free, dependent on no other man, and the actual 'begetting' is left to God.[35] So he rejoices, in spite of his keen sense of humiliation, because *The Corsair* has made it possible for him to sustain this relationship. He explains in his journal:

At the present time I am situated as correctly as possible in literature from the ideological point of view, and at the same time situated in such a way that to be an author becomes an action. The idea of breaking with *The Corsair* in order to prevent any direct approach, just when I had finished with [the pseudonymous] authorship and, by acknowledging all the pseudonyms, ran the risk of becoming a sort of authority, was a very happy thought. Furthermore, at the same moment that I come out polemically against the age, I owe it to the idea and to irony to prevent any possible confusion with the ironical bad spirits with which *The Corsair* attends on the dance floor of vulgarity. And here once again, as so often before, something more results which, in spite of all my reflection, is not due to me but to Providence. The things which I do after the greatest possible consideration, I so often understand far better afterwards,

[35] *Philosophical Fragments,* translated with Introduction by David F. Swenson, second ed, revised by Howard V. Hong with Introduction and Commentary by Niels Thulstrup (Princeton University Press, 1962; Cf. Oxford Univesity Press edition, 1962), p. 38.

not only their ideological significance but the fact that that was exactly what I should have done.[36]

Kierkegaard's journal continued to the end of his life to reflect this intense concern that his own position on the stage should be consonant with the purpose of his writings at the time. This preoccupation was carried so far that the modern reader of the journal may be excused for finding quite pathological all the private intrigues in which it involved him. To Kierkegaard himself, however, this intriguing was supported by Providence and was required of him as a 'spy in the highest service'.[37] Like other spies and conspirators, he drew heavily on the arts of the stage. This kinship of his own task to the theatrical arts, in turn, doubtless sharpened his perceptiveness as a spectator in the theatre.

v. *Crisis in the Life of a Christian Author*

Kierkegaard allowed *The Crisis* to be published only after the most tortuous inner debate. His reluctance did not have the grounds that one might expect in an author. He was proud enough of the piece, and he certainly was not the man to shrink from unleashing its sharp polemics. Yet the finished article lay unpublished for at least a year. When in the early summer of 1848 he finally began to consider seriously whether or not to publish it, he drew up a little list of pros and cons in his journal. First, there were some personal reasons for wishing to do so, e.g. he wanted both to honour Fru Heiberg and to provoke her husband a bit. But the most serious consideration was the following:

I have devoted myself exclusively to the religious for so

---

[36] *Journals*, 588. Cf. *The Point of View*, p. 58.
[37] Ibid., 791.

long that people will perhaps attempt to make it seem that
I have undergone a change, that I have grown very serious
(which I formerly was not), that the literary attack [by *The
Corsair*] has made me pious; in short, where my religion is
concerned people will make out that it is the kind of thing
one falls back on as one gets older. That is a heresy which
I consider it of the utmost importance to fight against. The
central nerve of my work as an author really lies in the fact
that I was essentially religious when I wrote *Either/Or*. I
therefore thought that it might be useful to exhibit that
possibility once again. I believe that my task lies precisely
in always being able to produce what the vanity and world-
liness of the world longs for as its highest, from which point
of view they proudly look down upon the religious as something suitable for those who have gone to seed – in always
being able, but not essentially willing. The world is so weak
that when it believes that a man who serves the religious is
not able to achieve the aesthetic it then looks down on the
religious.

That is a very important reason *pro*. But now *contra*. I
have now embarked so decisively upon Christianity, have
presented much of it so strictly and seriously, that there are
certainly people who have been influenced along that direction. Now it might almost be a scandal to them to hear that
I had written about an actress in a supplement. And indeed
one has a responsibility toward them.[38]

Furthermore, it had been Kierkegaard's practice to publish a
religious work under his own name along with any aesthetic or
pseudonymous writing, and 'at the present moment I have no
religious work printed which could appear at the same time'.
So he decides against publishing the piece.

---

[38] Ibid., 795. I have revised Dru's translation of this passage somewhat. The original is printed in *Søren Kierkegaards Papirer*, IX, 175.

This little debate provides an extreme example of the extent to which Kierkegaard's religious motivations could express themselves in a fundamentally theatrical way. The act of publishing an article is regarded, quite independent of the value of the work itself, as a gesture whose effect on his audience had to be carefully calculated. 'I would rather write a folio than publish a page,' he exclaims while embroiled in this debate. Even he came to feel that his scruples in this case had been exaggerated. To the passage quoted above he later attached a *nota bene*:

N.B. This is what is conceited about the whole affair; it is reflection which wants to make me extraordinarily self-important, instead of having confidence in God and being what I am.

As we shall see, he finally did resolve in this matter to have confidence in God and be what he was. But the debate, reflected in several journal entries, was painful and protracted.

We have noticed that Kierkegaard had written many aesthetic works previously, indeed that the whole pseudonymous authorship had been aesthetic in the broad sense, without his ever having been overcome by religious scruples. But during those earlier years he had utilized the aesthetic with a design in mind, the ultimate purpose of which was the service of Christianity. Now the situation had changed. The publication of the *Postscript* in 1846 had marked the turning-point, for it had brought the earlier design to its fulfilment.[39] Since

---

[39] In speaking of the pseudonymous authorship as having had a 'design' I am assuming the interpretation which Kierkegaard gave, after the fact, in *The Point of View*. To speak of a design, however, is not to imply that Kierkegaard had a detailed blueprint before him from the outset, that his thought was fully elaborated and the books definitely planned, and only awaited being put on paper. Kierkegaard was able, retrospectively, to make the design, and the ingenius 'deception' of the aesthetic works, seem more fully calculated than they probably were when he was actually carrying out the project.

then the explicitly religious discourse had predominated, and both the topics and the point of view had become more and more strictly and directly Christian. In 1847 his *Edifying Discouses in a Different Vein* were produced, really three books which 'reduplicate' the three ways of life from a religious point of view: *Consider the Lilies, Purity of Heart,* and *The Gospel of Suffering.* Later that year *The Works of Love* appeared, another very large book. *Christian Discourses* were published in April 1848. Meanwhile he was writing and re-writing his big *Book on Adler,* not a book of discourses this time but a more technical theological work aptly titled *On Authority and Revelation* in the English translation. During these years he actually surpassed the astonishing productivity of his earlier years, and still had a large body of distinctively Christian discourses in prospect.

Now, what could be the justification for publishing the little

---

He admits as much himself, suggesting that the design must essentially be attributed to divine 'Governance'. 'For in case I were to affirm out and out that from the very first instant I had a survey of the whole authorship, or that at every moment, stage by stage, I had by anticipation so far exhausted the possibilities that later reflection had not taught me anything, not even this other thing, that though what I had done was surely right, yet only afterwards was I in a position to understand thoroughly that this was so – if I were to do this, it would be a denial of God and dishonesty towards Him.' Rather, 'it is Governance that has educated me, and the education is reflected in the process of the productivity. In view of this it must be admitted that what I set forth above about the whole aesthetic production being a deceit is not quite true, for this expression assumes a little too much in the way of consciousness. At the same time, however, it is not altogether false, for I had been conscious of being under instruction, and that from the very first. The process is this: a poetic and philosophic nature is put aside in order to become a Christian. But the unusual feature is that the two movements begin simultaneously, and hence this is a conscious process, one is able to perceive how it comes about, the second movement does not supervene after a series of years. . . . The religious is present from the very first instant and has a decisive predominance' (*The Point of View*, pp. 72–74). This corrected interpretation of the design of the pseudonymous authorship is generally supported by the journal entries written while it was in process.

essay on Fru Heiberg? He had probably written it as a kind of diversion from his heavy religious writings, and plainly wanted to publish it. But this piece could not serve the same purpose as the earlier aesthetic writings, since that purpose had been fulfilled. It is significant that he does feel that publication of the little work has to be justified, and justified religiously. Yet his general position about the relation of the religious to the aesthetic would not seem to imply that an aesthetic work must be religiously justified. Why, indeed, had he felt the need to give a religious rationale for the earlier aesthetic production? Granted that in a particular case an aesthetic production might have an ultimately religious purpose, does it need such a purpose before a religious man may engage in it? Kierkegaard seems ambivalent regarding this question. But he would have denied that any general answer to it is possible, at least any general answer which is absolutely binding. Precisely the religious man is set apart as an 'individual', singled out by God for his own unique calling. General principles – i.e. ethical principles, since it is the ethical which claims universality in guiding human conduct – cannot simply be set aside; even the man of faith may be given some 'general' guidance. But he cannot make his own decision by a simple deduction from a general principle, for example regarding the proper relation of faith to aesthetics. He must respond to his own calling in his own unique situation. The long debate over the publication of *The Crisis* is an example of the seriousness with which Kierkegaard took the responsibility of his vocation as an author whose work was to be under divine commission.

In fact, it appears likely that Kierkegaard's dilemma regarding publication of this piece was not fully expressed in the reasons which he offers pro and con in his explicit discussion of the matter, but had its source in a profound personal crisis regarding his vocation. There are many hints in the journals which point to this much deeper inner debate during this period. In January of 1847, when he was still considering the possibility of bringing his writing to a close and taking up a post in official Christendom as a country parson, he was deterred by a sense that something was demanded of him on the larger scene which he ought not evade by flight to a rural parsonage. *'Conditions here are becoming more and more confused,'* he writes in his journal. He is certain 'that literary, social, and political conditions require an *extraordinarius'*, and 'the question now is whether there is anyone in the kingdom besides myself who is fitted for the work'.[40] This was doubtless the most momentous and even dreadful question that Kierkegaard could possibly have posed to himself, and could have led to a radical break with his former role.

During this period and for the next couple of years his mind was deeply occupied with the idea of the *extraordinarius*. The *extraordinarius* in his view is the 'witness to the Truth' in the most eminent degree, the direct bearer of a fresh divine word. He is a prophet or apostle, set aside by God for a great and absolutely unique mission, and therefore an exception to any of the normal categories of life. Kierkegaard's exploration of this special role finds its clearest expression in the *Book on Adler* (*On Authority and Revelation*). Though this work was not published in his lifetime, he did publish a crucial passage from it in 1849, entitled 'The Difference Between a Genius and an Apostle',[41] as one of *Two Minor Ethico–Religious Discourses*. The apostle is seized by God, and serves exclusively the divine command which has been addressed to him and of which he is the bearer. He speaks with authority, without appeal to human wisdom; his categories are transcendent, and therefore his word is inherently and irreducibly paradoxical from the standpoint of any possible human reflection.

---

[40] *Journals*, 626.
[41] Published as a separate essay in the Harper Torchbooks edition of *The Present Age*. See also *On Authority and Revelation*, translated by Walter Lowrie (Oxford University Press, 1953, and Princeton University Press, 1955), pp. 103ff.

But the genius is 'without authority' and 'remains in the sphere
of reflection'. Even when he propounds apparent paradoxes, it
is only because he is ahead of his time or of superior discern-
ment. His paradoxes may be difficult to understand, but they
are not essentially beyond human understanding. The contrast
is further suggested by the affinity of the *extraordinarius* with
the martyr, who is also a 'witness to the Truth', discussed in
the other 'Minor Ethico–Religious' discourse which raises the
question, 'Has a Man the Right to let Himself be put to
Death for the Truth?' He answers that the ordinary man, and
even the ordinary Christian, cannot presume to follow Christ
to this extreme point; only one specially called has the right to
be a martyr. So also with the *extraordinarius*, who may, in
fact, be a martyr as well; certainly for Kierkegaard himself
the possibility of the extraordinary calling also involved the
possibility of martyrdom.

Kierkegaard had known himself to be a genius; he indulged
in no blushing modesty on that point. Certainly he had considered himself an exception, in virtue of his physical frailty,
his abysmal melancholy, his remarkable intellectual and poetic
powers. This sense of being an exception had driven him to
break his engagement and renounce the ethical norm of marriage, and now it demanded that he renounce his fond wish to
accept an office in the Church. Moreover, he had devoted his
genius to the service of Christianity, and had a keen sense of
divine 'Governance' guiding his work as an author. As such he
was certainly a rarity. But then the actress whom he discusses
in *The Crisis* is also said to be an exception, in virtue of her
genius (see p. 88 below). People endowed with special gifts
and special dedication are exceptional, and 'the individual' in
the religious sense is still more exceptional, but none of them
is as such *the* exception in the strictest sense. Even the 'godly
poet', who cannot evade the insistent marginal notation to go
and do likewise, yet does not have his life brought under the
divine yoke with the terrible simplicity and intensity of the

extraordinarius. Just as he feared he would be Kierkegaard is sometimes called a prophet today, but he repeatedly and strenuously objected to being given any such title. Hence the almost ritualistic use in the prefaces to his religious works of the reminder that he writes 'without authority'. He was only attempting to evoke in a fresh way the sense of what it meant to be a Christian, something which had already been known and was still known in a routine and therefore diminished way. In an age in which being a Christian was taken for granted, that had been task enough, requiring the utmost of his poetic and dialectical powers. That had been the extent of his vocation. In 'a word about myself', written in his journal in 1847, he says :

> I occupy the extreme position in the poetic spectrum which is just short of being a sort of reformer on a small scale. I have much more imagination than such a man would have, but then again less of a certain personal power which is needed in order to appear in that way. With the help of my imagination (which, be it noted, is not of the immediate sort which would take precedence over the dialectical, but follows the lead of the dialectical) I can grasp all the Christian qualifications with the greatest precision and vividness. The times clearly require that. There are certain things which must continually be called to mind or otherwise the standard is lost. It is like the flight of wild birds above the heads of tame ones when those qualifications of the Christian life are recalled which demand the utmost. But just because I am a poet in that sense, one whose task is to raise the price and if possible whisper to every individual what the demands could be, I must take particular care not to acquire any followers.[42]

---

[42] *Journals,* 704. I have revised Dru's translation considerably. See *Søren Kierkegaards Papirer,* VIII A, 347.

Yet the times now seemed to demand an *extraordinarious*. Of course, only God, and not the times, could bring such a one into existence. But Kierkegaard writes in his journal, on 16 August, 1847, that 'something is stirring within me which points to a metamorphosis'.[43] It seemed to him during this period that God was establishing a new kind of relationship to him, which might issue in a new task. But he was uncertain. Perhaps the most striking expression of this crisis of vocation is contained in a passage in *The Sickness unto Death*, on which he was already at work in the spring of 1848. The passage is clearly autobiographical; it has many echoes in the journals during this time, though the journal entries are seldom so frank or so clear. He is discussing 'a poet-existence in the direction of the religious' at 'the most dialectical border-line between despair and sin'. The problem of this poet-existence is that it is passionately related to God, but the relationship is expressed primarily in imagination and not yet decisively in existence. From a Christian standpoint this is 'the sin of poeticizing instead of being' before God. As a poet of religious existence he knows that God could resolve his despair, yet as a man he clings to the despair and therefore cannot give himself over to faith. Yet he entertains the possibility that this impasse may be preparing him to be singled out for the extraordinary calling:

With respect to the religious he is an unhappy lover, that is, he is not in a strict sense a believer, he has only the first prerequisite of faith: despair, and with that an ardent longing for the religious. His collision is essentially this: is he one who is being called, is the thorn in the flesh the expression for the fact that he is to be used for the extra-ordinary, is it before God quite as it should be with respect

[43] *Journals*, 694.

to the extraordinary figure he has become? or is the thorn in the flesh that under which he must humble himself in order to attain the universal human? But enough of this. I can say with the emphasis of truth, 'To whom am I talking?' Who will bother about such psychological investigations carried to the *nth* power?[44]

It is clear enough to whom he is talking. The poet-existence has been called radically into question, has become a burden and an inhibition to him. A metamorphosis is stirring, but it is not yet clear what God means to make of him. Is he to receive a 'normal' vocation, and so cease being the exception which he has been, or is he to become the exception *par excellence*? In either case he believes that his enclosure in reflection, his melancholy, his self-isolation will finally be overcome.

The metamorphosis which he had already felt stirring in 1847 appeared to be brought to birth during Holy Week, 1848. In the journal entry for Wednesday, April 19, he declares:

My whole being is changed. My concealment and self-isolation [*Indesluttethed* – 'closed-in-ness'] is broken – I must speak.
Lord give thy grace.

It is impossible to know exactly what is implied in this outcry, what new possibility seemed to open itself to him. He had already resolved to abandon the Socratic, indirect form of address in favour of some kind of direct testimony to the Gospel and direct relationship with his fellow-men. At least he means to go off the stage, and speak in his own person. What form this speaking might take is obscure, but a new vocation

[44] *The Sickness Unto Death*, tr. Walter Lowrie (Princeton University Press, 1941, and Oxford University Press, 1942), pp. 123–26 (Doubleday Anchor edition, 1954, pp. 208–10,. I have revised Lowrie's translation.

seems in prospect. Yet there were second thoughts. The following Monday he says, 'No, no, my self-isolation cannot be thrown off, at least not now. The thought of throwing it off occupies me so greatly and so constantly that it only sets in more and more firmly.'[45] He has a keener sense of the forgiveness of sins, by which he might be released; but he has not yet received a full sense of the release. He adds that 'If my self-isolation is to be broken it will more probably happen by God helping me in some way or other into a regular calling in life.' The possibility of the country parish or something of the sort has been revived. But that was evidently not what Kierkegaard had had in mind a few days before, when he felt that his whole being had changed, had felt at once freed and compelled to speak in a sense in which he had not spoken before. What remained from the experience during the weeks that followed it was an overwhelming sense of the love of God, and a vivid hope that a metamorphosis might yet occur.

And now, now that in many ways I have been brought to the last extremity, now (since last Easter, though with intervals) a hope has awakened in my soul that God may desire to resolve the fundamental misery of my being. That is to say, now I am in faith in the profoundest sense. Faith is immediacy after reflection. As poet and thinker I have represented all things in the medium of the imagination, myself living in resignation. Now life comes closer to me, or I am closer to myself, coming to myself.[46]

---

[45] *Journals*, 747, 749. I have revised Dru's translation in both cases. See *Søren Kierkegaards Papirer*, VIII A, 640, 645.

[46] *Journals*, 754. During that Holy Week Kierkegaard had written: 'Considered poetically, immediacy is that to which one wishes to return (one wishes his childhood back, etc.), but from a Christian standpoint immediacy is lost, and it is not to be *wished* back but grasped again . . . in a certain sense Christianity by comparison with poetry . . . is prosaic – and yet it is precisely the poetry of eternity.' *Papirer*, VIII A, 643 (not included in Dru's selection from the journals).

On the other hand, the conviction seized him that he was going to die soon.[47]

At any rate, the question about his future role was not yet decisively answered, but continued to burden his mind. Now the question arose whether to publish *The Crisis*. In the light of his inner turmoil the anxious brooding about this question becomes more understandable. Even if Kierkegaard did not seriously entertain the possibility that he might be brought forth in the role of the *extraordinarius* – for whom any flirtation with the aesthetic would be impossible – still his vocation was now in such a state of uncertainty that he must beware of making any false moves.

But shortly after he had decided not to publish *The Crisis* he changed his mind.

No, no, the little article must appear. It is nothing but melancholy reflection in which I have become entangled. Lately the thought of dying soon has been constantly with me and I have therefore written and written, continuously, in the hope that it would only be published after my death. Then the thought of publishing the little article occurred to me; it means so much to me; Gjødwad turned up at the same time [publisher of *The Fatherland* who had been coaxing him for an article]; I trust to that as though it were a providential sign – and then, then my melancholy reflection transformed what was unquestionably a trifle, an innocent thing, a little pleasure I had hoped to have the pleasure of giving a few people – that is what my melancholy reflection transformed into something so tremendous that it seemed as though I should scandalize people and cut myself

[47] In fact, Kierkegaard later reveals that part of his reluctance to publish *The Crisis* had stemmed from his fear that it might be the last of his works to appear, and he did not wish to end on that note. *Papirer*, IX, 219 (not included in Dru's selection).

off from God. It is neither more nor less than indolence and melancholy. . . .

And now, as far as giving scandal is concerned, above all things let me not pass myself off as being more religious than I am, nor risk falling prey to any form of exaggerated pietism. I was ready to answer to God for writing it – well, now I can, I shall publish it, for I must be honest. I should certainly not write anything of the kind again – but then, too, it is an old work. (That is why the article is dated: Summer 1847, and consequently all that anxious doubt dismissed.)

In God's name, then – oh, it is so difficult to use God's name in connection with such trifles. But the thing that really matters is being true to myself, having the frankness to be myself before God and of accepting everything from his hands.

And perhaps it will all end as I began, in my being pleased at having done as I did.[48]

In fact Kierkegaard became very pleased indeed with his decision. He continued discussing the decision through several more journal entries, and returned to it from time to time for months thereafter, rejoicing that he had indeed published the piece.[49] He even considered reproducing it in a book, along with other articles. For the resolution to publish the article was a momentous one in his personal life. It represented a new acceptance, with perhaps a new style of address, of his old vocation as a poet in the service of the Gospel. If the publication of the religious writings should make people forget that he is essentially a poet, the article on the theatre would remind them.

---

[48] *Journals*, 796. Fortunately even his resolution never to produce anything of the sort again was revoked, by his writing the article on Phister later that year.
[49] Ibid., 796–800. See *Papirer*, IX, 178–81, 184, 186–87, 189, 219, 227–29, 455.

After having made his decision, he especially takes himself to task in his journals for having taken seriously the consideration that he might give offence to people who had been helped by his religious writings. This had been only a momentary thought, 'which is quite foreign to me, antagonistic to the very thing which I must describe as the central point in my position as one serving Christianity'.[50] For the point had been that the whole authorship, including its aesthetic phase, was religiously motivated from beginning to end. And therefore, 'the illusion that I flew to Christianity because I was no longer capable of moving about and disporting myself in aesthetics is one which cannot be allowed to pass'.[51] Now he is able to see the article as rounding out his authorship as a whole. It will stand as a faint musical echo of the aesthetic works with which the authorship began, just as the early Edifying Discourses had furnished a premonition of the explicitly religious works which were to come. Both in the piece 'On My Work as an Author', which he published in 1851, and in *The Point of View for My Work as an Author*, which he wrote in 1848 and was published posthumously, he gives this significance to the little article.

Coming at the beginning, the *Two Edifying Discourses* had hinted, like a preliminary flash, that this [the religious] was really what was to come out of it all, the goal to be attained. The flash of the little aesthetic article, coming as it does at the conclusion, by reflecting as it were the hint given at the beginning of the authorship, draws attention to the fact that from the very beginning the aesthetic was merely the point of departure, a position which had to be left behind.[52]

[50] Ibid., 797.
[51] Ibid., 798.
[52] 'On My Work as an Author', published with *The Point of View*, p. 150. See also *The Point of View*, p. 14.

In both of these little books on his work as an author, Kierkegaard stresses the religious intent of the authorship as a whole. That is the main point, but there is another point to be noticed, minor by comparison but still of great significance to Kierkegaard himself. If *The Crisis* testifies to the religious intent of the whole authorship in the oblique way suggested, it also testifies rather more directly to the fact that the author remains a poet. In a footnote to 'On My Work as an Author', in commenting on his essay on 'The Difference between a Genius and an Apostle', he again underlines this difference and accepts the application to his own work which must be drawn from it:

> Genius as such remains in the sphere of reflection. That again is the category of my whole authorship: to *call attention* to the religious, more specifically to Christianity – but *without authority*.[53]

Again, he states the matter succinctly in a journal entry dating from 1849:

> Mohammed protests with all his might against being called a poet and the Koran a poem. I protest with all my might against being looked upon as a prophet and only desire to be a poet.[54]

This means, as he often says, that he is merely an 'ordinary Christian'. He has a Christian vocation as an author, but it is only such as any 'ordinary Christian' might have, who possessed his human qualifications. No doubt Kierkegaard continued to ponder the problem of his vocation, but he never essentially revised this view of the matter. In the spectacular 'Attack upon Christendom', which he launched in the last year of his life, he certainly assumed a new role, public, violent,

[53] Ibid., p. 147.
[54] Journals., 885.

and direct as a whiplash. But he claimed no transcendent authorization for his attack. He still spoke 'without authority' and denied being a prophet or reformer, or the founder of a new order. In declaring Christendom to be a perversion of New Testament Christianity, his only basis was evidence available to every 'ordinary Christian' and the only demand was for common human honesty in the matter.

Publishing *The Crisis* represented an important personal decision. If he had ever seriously considered the possibility that he might be a witness to the Truth in the extraordinary sense, the question was now resolved in his own mind and he was sure that he had appeared on the stage in the right costume, without passing himself off as 'more religious' than he was. Shortly after publishing the piece, he reflects how fortunate he was that he had done so:

If I had died without doing so I am quite sure that some people would have come forward with all the confused notions of our times and have talked nonsense about my being an apostle. Good God, instead of helping to make Christianity honoured I should have ruined it. A charming affinity, indeed for apostles – for me too to be an apostle. And as the fruit of my life to have helped to establish in men's minds the masterly thought: that I too was a sort of apostle.

I have watched for that terrible confusion with the eyes of a lynx. In such a muddle-headed time as ours, one which flirts with everything – if it only sets eyes on someone who differs somewhat from the parsons – oh, it is so easy to cause confusion. Was not that the ambition of Magister Adler? I have tried to prevent it with fear and trembling. Hence my constant use of the expression: without authority; hence the treatise: 'On the Difference between a Genius and an Apostle.' But all that would not have helped – but now an article about an actress.

Personally, as a man, I am a poor wretch whom a melancholy old man made as unhappy as possible out of love – one whom God then took charge of and for whom he has done 'so indescribably, oh, so indescribably much more than I ever expected,' oh, so indescribably much more that I only long for the peace of eternity in order to do nothing but thank him. As a man, personally, I am, in a more general sense, a sinner who has been far along the road to perdition, whose conversion was only too often and is often marked by relapses – a sinner who nevertheless believes that all his sins are forgiven him for Christ's sake, even though he must bear the result of punishment; a sinner who longs for eternity in order to thank Him and His love.[55]

In publishing an article about an actress, Kierkegaard renounced all claim to be anything but an 'ordinary Christian'. But by the single-mindedness with which he carried out his task of becoming an ordinary Christian he showed just how extraordinary the life of an ordinary Christian must be; and that was the fundamental intention of all his work.

[55] Ibid., 800.

THE CRISIS
AND
A CRISIS IN THE LIFE OF AN ACTRESS

by *Inter et Inter*[1]

published in four parts
in *The Fatherland*
July 24–27, 1848

THE CRISIS AND
A CRISIS IN THE LIFE OF AN ACTRESS

I

I suppose that when most people think of an actress of the first rank they imagine her condition in life to be so enchanting and brilliant that they generally quite forget its thorny side: the incredibly many trivialities and all the unfairness or misunderstanding just at the critical moment that an actress may have to contend with.

Let us conceive of the most favourable situation possible. Let us imagine an actress who possesses everything she needs in order to be absolutely of the first rank; let us suppose that she wins admiration and acclaim, and that she is fortunate enough (and this is undoubtedly a great stroke of fortune) not to become the target for one or another spiteful person's persecution. So she lives on year after year, envied, successful, the perpetual object of open admiration. That seems just splendid; it looks as though that would really be something. But when one looks closer and discovers the sort of coin in which this open admiration is paid, discovers the poor sum of shabby trivialities which in the world of the theatre critics constitutes the fund *ad usus publicos*[2] (and it is indeed from this fund that the constant open admiration is regularly paid), then it does seem just possible that even the most fortunate situation for an actress is shoddy and poor enough. However true it may be, as one hears, that the wardrobe of the Royal Theatre is very costly and precious, one thing is certain: that the wardrobe of the newspaper critics is appallingly shabby.

Further. The admired artist lives on, then, year after year. Just as in a bourgeois household one knows beforehand exactly what the dinner menu will be for each day, so she knows beforehand exactly what the season has in store for her. Two or three times each week she will be praised and admired, deafened with applause; already within the first three months she will more than once have undergone the newspaper critic's total repertoire of platitudes and – turns of phrase, as they can with special emphasis be called, since the same phrases keep turning up. Once or twice, or in good years three times, she will be celebrated in the song of one or another dissipated good-for-nothing or would-be poet. Her portrait will be painted for every art exhibit; she will be lithographed, and if her luck runs very high her portrait will even be printed on handkerchiefs and the crowns of hats. And she, who as a woman is sensitive regarding her name – as only a woman is sensitive – she knows that her name is on everyone's lips, even when they wipe their mouths with their handkerchiefs! She knows that she is the subject of everyone's admiring conversation, including those who are in the utmost distress for something to chatter about. She lives on in this way year after year. That seems just splendid; it looks as though that would really be something. But if in a higher sense she had to live on the rich nourishment of this admiration, take encouragement from it, receive strength and inspiration for renewed exertions – and since even the most highly talented person, and particularly a woman, can become despondent in a weak moment for want of some expression of genuine appreciation – at such a time she will really feel what she has doubtless realized often enough, just how fatuous all this is, and what a mistake it is to envy her this burdensome splendour.[3]

Meanwhile, as the years go by, though not many in these prying and impatient times, the prattle already begins to stir to the effect that she is now beginning to get older. And so – oh yes, we live in a Christian land, but just as one often enough sees examples of aesthetic brutishness, so also the cannibalistic lust for human sacrifice has by no means gone out of fashion in Christendom. The same intense vulgarity which had never

ceased beating the great drum of triviality in her praise and
honouring her fondly on the cymbals, this same vulgarity has
now become bored with the idolized artist. It wants to be rid
of her, wants her out of its sight; she can thank God that it
does not want her put to death. This same vulgarity has a new
sixteen-year-old idol, and in her honour the former idol must
feel vulgarity's full disfavour – for this is the great hardship
which is involved in being an idol, that it is all but unthinkable that one should be allowed to resign this position in
honour. Even if this does not happen, and nothing quite so
crude is perpetrated, still something else sometimes happens,
which seems much better but basically is just as bad. In this
case the vulgar triviality is flowing along so briskly from the
earlier admiration that the idol, even after she has grown older
(as people express it), may still be carried along on its
momentum for a while. No obvious change is observed in
vulgarity's effusions concerning the idolized artist; yet one
seems to detect a certain hesitancy, which betrays the fact that
the worshipful Rosiflengius rather fancies that he has performed a service for the artist, that he is being *gallant* in
continuing to say the same things. But to be gallant towards
an artist is precisely the highest degree of insolence, a maudlin
impertinence and a disgusting kind of intrusiveness. Anyone
who is something, and is something essentially, poses *eo ipso*
the claim to be recognized for exactly this special thing, and
for nothing more nor less. If, as they say, the theatre is a
sacred place, at least it is profaned often enough. How burdensome and painful in one's sixteenth year to have to endure
hypocritical genuflections and declarations of love in the form
of art criticism from bald and half-witted old reviewers; and
how bitter later on to have to put up with the impudence of
gallantry!

But now what is the reason for this inhumanity which
directs so much injustice and even cruelty against women
dedicated to the service of art? What reason except that

aesthetic cultivation is so rare among people. Where the feminine is concerned, most people's appreciation of art is in its essential categories and its way of thinking like that of every butcher's apprentice, officer of the guard, or store–clerk, who talks enthusiastically about a damn pretty or a devil of a lively wench of eighteen. These eighteen years, this damnable prettiness and this devilish liveliness, that is the art-appreciation – and also its brutishness. On the other hand, when the aesthetic interest really begins, when inwardness comes into its own and is revealed with intensive significance in the metamorphosis: then the mass of people lose interest. If one does continue to admire, it means that one intends to be gallant or indulgent; for when she is only thirty years old she is essentially *passé*.

It is really to be wished, especially for people's own sakes, so that they would not be deprived or would not deprive themselves of the richest enjoyments, that this prejudice could be thoroughly eradicated. And it really is a prejudice, indeed a brutish prejudice, for a woman does not become an actress in her eighteenth year. She is more likely to become one in her thirtieth year or later, if she becomes one at all; for this play-acting in the eighteenth year is aesthetically of dubious merit. It is so far from gallantry to begin admiring an actress in the later period of her development, that the opposite is really the flattery: to admire a little girl of sixteen. I cannot believe that an essentially cultivated aesthetician could bring himself to make a sixteen-year-old actress the subject of a critique, especially if she were very pretty, etc. He would doubtless avoid such an ambiguous situation. True, it will often happen that one who has created a furore as a young girl never does come through. Maybe so, but then she has never essentially been an actress but has created a furore on the stage entirely in the same sense that a young girl creates a furore in social circles for one or two winters. On the other hand, it is also true that when the metamorphosis is successful there can be no talk of gallantry, for only then is admiration, aesthetically understood, really appropriate.

Of course, much is done for the actresses in the theatre to secure their future. I think it would also be very beneficial if this utterly unaesthetic superstition about the eighteen years could be done away with, and if it could be made quite clear that the most decisive juncture occurs much later – this, too, would provide a safeguard for the actresses' future. And the matter itself has not only an aesthetic, but also a great psychological interest. Indeed, I am surprised that it has not more often been made a subject for reflection. The interesting thing is to be able, in a purely aesthetic way but with the aid of psychology, to anticipate the metamorphosis or at least to explain it when it has set in.

However, a short article in a newspaper is not the suitable place for a detailed investigation into several cases. I shall merely attempt here, in a purely psychological and aesthetic manner, to describe one metamorphosis, certainly a difficult one but just for that reason one that is also beautiful and significant. For the more that has been devoted and the more that has therefore been committed to the first phase, the harder it is to develop a new phase. And the more an essentially unaesthetic public has given idolizing and noisy attention to the first, the easier it is for the attitude of that same public to be transformed into an anxious, distrustful, even sullen opposition to the metamorphosis. An actress who has never had the luck to be in unquestionable possession of that which so greatly captivates and enchants the unaesthetic spectators may as a compensation be lucky enough to enact her metamorphosis in all quietness. That, too, is beautiful, and precisely because it takes place so quietly. But it is also easier, simply because the quiet transformation leading up to the metamorphosis is neither ruined by inquisitiveness nor disturbed by misunderstanding, but is withdrawn from the whims of the public. For the public is peculiar. When in the course of ten years, for example, time has taken the liberty of making the acknowledged favourite ten years older: then the public gets angry – with the favourite.

II

So I am imagining an actress at the very beginning of her career, in the first triumph of her early youth, at the moment when she appears for the first time, and for the first time scores a brilliant success. It is aesthetically correct for me to speak of this situation, and to speak of it with pleasure, because my investigation is of an ideal sort and not concerned with any contemporary actress of sixteen. It is aesthetically proper for me to speak of such a youthful beginning for another reason as well: since the subject of this investigation is the metamorphosis itself, I am not concerned in this essay with her youthful phase as such. The portrayal of the first phase is for the sake of laying the groundwork, it is poetically and philosophically a recollection, but quite without sadness. We do not linger over the first phase, but rather hasten beyond it, since one always hastens on to that which is higher, and the author is aesthetically convinced that the metamorphosis is the highest.

She makes her début, then, in her seventeenth year. She is in possession of – well, what it is that she possesses is very difficult to define, just because it is something indeterminate, which nevertheless asserts itself overwhelmingly and demands an unconditional response. There is no use in even the dullest, most peevish person hardening himself against it, he must respond. Take a mathematician. He may rear up on his hind legs and demands to know what that proves, but it is no use, he must respond, at heart he is convinced: *ergo* she is in possession of – well, what it is that she possesses is very difficult to define, just because it is something indeterminate. It is astonishing. In other cases you can usually specify exactly what quality a person possesses, and when you have done that, then again you can see exactly how much that person is doing with – whatever he possesses. But on the contrary, a young actress who possesses this indefinable quality instantly makes all mere property-owners appear poor by comparison.

But to come a little closer to defining this indefinable possession, let us call it: *Luck*. She is in possession of luck. Luck does not signify here that she is fortunate enough to have good friends and influential connections, or fortunate enough to be engaged by the theatre on profitable terms, or so fortunate as to have the director and critics interested in her. No, luck signifies here what Caesar meant when he said to the ship captain: you are carrying Caesar – and his luck.[4] Indeed, were it not for the fact that she would be tempting her luck, she might rashly dare each evening she plays to have printed on the playbill: Miss N. N. and her luck – to that degree is she in possession of luck. It is not merely that luck is on her side, though it is already a great deal that this almighty power is pleased to escort a young girl; but the luck is even at her beck and call.[5] If she cannot be said to possess this luck, it is only because she is possessed by it. It attends her wherever she goes and wherever she stops, in everything she undertakes, in the least movement of her hand, in every wink of her eye or toss of her head, in every turn of her figure, in her motion, in her voice, in her facial expression. In short, luck dances attendance on her to such a degree that the sensitive critic is not permitted to detect, even for a second, what she would be like apart from her luck, even if he is already aesthetically aware of the extent to which the best aspects of her artistry do not in another sense belong to her at all.

To come still a little closer to defining her indefinable possession, let us further call it: *Youthfulness*. This is not to be taken in the statistical sense, that she completed her sixteenth year a week ago Monday. Nor does it mean that she is a young girl who is put on display because of such things as her beauty, and to that extent cannot properly be called an

actress at all.[6] No, her youthfulness is again an indefinable
treasure. First and foremost, it is the play of vital powers,
what one could also call the vivacious, abundant restlessness
of youth, of which one always speaks with spontaneous affection, as when it is said that a happily gifted child is the restless
one in the family. Of course, you can soon have enough of
restlessness, in the sense of finitude run riot. But restlessness
in the pregnant sense, the restlessness of infinity,[7] the joyous,
vivacious originality which stirs the waters with rejuvenating,
refreshing, healing powers, such restlessness signifies something further, something very great: it signifies the first flaring
of an essential genius. And this restlessness is nothing fortuitous, it does not mean simply that she cannot stand still. On
the contrary, it means hat even when she does stand still one
intuits this restlessness in her very repose. It does not mean
that she comes running on to the stage, but means on the
contrary that when she merely moves one can detect the
swiftness of infinity. It does not mean that she speaks so
rapidly that one cannot follow her, but means on the contrary
that even when she speaks quite slowly one is able to sense the
animation of her breath and spirit. This restlessless does not
imply that she must quickly tire, but just the opposite: it reveals an elemental tirelessness, like the wind or the sounds of
nature. It reveals that her playfulness is inexhaustibly rich,
that it only hints at how much more she possesses. It reveals
that her coquetry (and such a personality utterly without
coquetry is unthinkable) is nothing but an exuberant and
innocent mind's happy, triumphant consciousness of its
indescribable luck. It is therefore not really coquetry, but
something that encourages the spectator still further; that is,
it assures him of the reliability of the whole performance,
makes him absolutely certain that her exuberance is secure.

It may be supposed that reliability on the one hand, and on
the other playfulness, liveliness, luck, youthfulness, are utterly
incongruous qualities that do not belong together at all. Yet

that is by no means the case; they do absolutely belong together. If you cannot be perfectly sure of her playfulness and
liveliness, if you cannot absolutely rely on her to have enough
for herself and a dozen others besides, then her performance
is *eo ipso* a failure and the pleasure is essentially lost. One can
also recognize that these qualities are really inseparable from
the fact that one naturally responds to playfulness by associat-
ing it with reliability: as when an older but still sprightly man
says, with complete affection for a playful young girl, 'Goodness knows you can rely on that little lady!' He does not
say that she is playful but that she is reliable, and yet that is
also to say that she is playful. For this reliability is nothing he
has invented, since she elicits this expression from him by her
playfulness.

It may be supposed that exuberance on the one hand, and
absolute assurance on the other, are again heterogeneous
qualities which do not belong together at all, or which only
blockheadedness would think of putting together. And yet
they are quite inseparable, and it is the dialectic which brings
this combination about. Anything which is an elemental fact
of nature, and as such single and simple, must be absolutely
secure. Anything which is compound can exist with something
lacking; but something which is a single unit, an immediacy,
must be absolute, or, to say the same thing, it is absolute when-
ever it is such. A little exuberance is to be rejected as altogether unlovely. Real exuberance, therefore, precisely because
of its absolute assurance, has above all a soothing effect on
the spectator; though this perhaps eludes the attention of most
people, who suppose that anything exuberant has a stimulating
effect, which is true only of something artificially exuberant or
a little bit exuberant. Let us take an example from immediate
comedy, from whimsey. On a night when you see Rosenkilde[8]
come on the stage, as if straight from the infinite and with its
swiftness, possessed by all the whimsical muses, when at the
first sight of him you find yourself saying, 'Well, this evening

he's blowing up a regular storm': then you feel *eo ipso* indescribably soothed. You heave a sigh and settle down to relax; you assume a comfortable posture, as if you intended to remain sitting for a long time in the same position; you almost regret not having brought some food along, because the situation induces such trust and assurance, and therefore such tranquility, that you forget that it is only a matter of an hour in the theatre. While you laugh and laugh and quietly rejoice in the whimsical exuberance, you feel constantly soothed, indescribably convinced and lulled as it were by Rosenkilde's absolute assurance, because his whimsey gives you the impression that it can continue as long as you want. And if, on the contrary, a comedian in the immediate mode is not first and foremost absolutely soothing, if the spectator is just a little bit anxious for fear his whimsey may finally fall flat, then the enjoyment is essentially lost. It is usually said that a comedian must be able to make the audience laugh, but it might be better to say that he must first and foremost be able absolutely to soothe, and then the laugher will follow of itself. For real laughter, laughter that comes from the heart, does not result from being stimulated, but precisely from being soothed. So it is with exuberance also: it must above all soothe with its absolute assurance; that is to say, if it is truly present in an actress it functions primarily in an absolutely soothing way. It is in this tranquility, induced by her absolute assurance and trustworthiness, that the spectator gives himself over to the exuberance. You see, here it is again: Exuberance and trustworthiness seem a strange combination, and it is odd to say of exuberance that it is trustworthy; and yet it is correct, and is only a new expression for playfulness, for this trustworthy exuberance is precisely playfulness.

To come still a little closer to defining her indefinable possession, let us further call it: *Soulfulness*. This means that in the temper of her immediate passion she is attuned to thought and idea; that her still unreflective inwardness is essentially in league with ideality; that every touch of a thought or idea strikes a note, giving a full-toned resonance; that she is an original, specific sensitivity. In this way she relates herself expressively[9] to the playwright's words; but to herself she relates herself still further, in what might properly be called the tone modulated to each speech and the harmony modulated to the character as a whole. Not only does she take the author's words correctly off his lips, but she gives them back to him in such a way, in the accompanying sound of her playfulness and the self-awareness of her genius, that she seems to say in addition: Let me see you copy that.[10]

Her indefinable possession signifies finally: *that she is in the right rapport with the tension of the stage.* Every tension, according to the dialectic's own dialectic, can have two different effects. It can reveal the strain it creates, but it can also do the opposite, can conceal the strain; and not only conceal it, but constantly transform it, change and transfigure it into lightness. Thus the lightness is invisibly grounded in the strain produced by the tension, but this strain is neither seen nor suspected; only the lightness is revealed. A heavy object can weigh something down. But conversely, it can also conceal the fact that it is heavy, and express its heaviness in the opposite way, by lifting something up in the air. People usually talk as though one became light by casting off one's burdens, and this view of the matter is the basis for all trivial outlooks on life. But in a higher, poetic or philosophical sense, the opposite is the case: One becomes light by means of – heaviness. One swings up high and free by means of – a pressure. Thus the celestial bodies soar through space by means of a great weight; birds fly with the help of tremendous pressure: the light soaring of faith is aided by a prodigious heaviness; the highest upswinging of hope is aided precisely by hardship and the pressure of adversity. However, it lays a prodigious burden on a person to have to support the illusion of the stage and the weight of everyone's eyes. In the absence of a happy rapport, therefore, even the highest degree of professional skill cannot quite conceal the heaviness of the burden; but where the happy rapport is present, the heaviness of the burden is continually transformed into lightness. That is the way it is with the young actress. She is in her own element in the tension of the stage, just there does she become as light as a bird. It is precisely the weight that makes her light, and the pressure that swings her up so high. There is not a trace of anxiety. In the wings, she may be anxious, but on stage she is happy and light as a bird just set free; for only now, under the pressure, is she free and has received her freedom. That which manifests itself as anxiety when she is at home in her study or in the wings is not impotence, but quite the opposite. It is her elasticity which makes her anxious, just because there is no pressure on her. In the tension of the theatre this anxiety marvellously manifests itself as potency. The notion that an artist must not be anxious is in general very narrow-minded, and to be without anxiety is above all a false indication of artistic greatness. For the more powers he possesses, the greater is his anxiety so long as he is outside the tension which exactly corresponds to his powers. Suppose once that the force of nature which supports the heavenly bodies were personified, and imagine a situation in which it had been relieved of its task and were waiting to take it up again: it would be in the grip of the most deathly anxiety, and only at the moment it took up its burden would it become carefree and light. Hence, one of the greatest torments a human being can suffer is to have too great an elasticity in proportion to the tension of the little world in which he lives; such an unhappy person can never come to feel entirely free, just because he cannot get enough weight on him. The important thing is simply that there should be just enough anxiety, that so far as the actor is concerned it should be kept off-stage, and should never appear on-stage as it does with the person who is not anxious off-stage.[11]

Her *definable possession* is of course easy to specify. She has not only natural grace, but also training. She possesses, as a subordinate aspect of her art, the larger part of a dancer's whole stock-in-trade. Her diction is correct, exact; her voice is not abused, but cultivated, moulding the words with fullness and clarity and without shrieking or breaking, not keeping them to herself or for herself, but projecting them from herself without inhibition. She articulates superbly, even when she whispers. She knows how to use the voice, and nothing testifies more to her qualifications than the way she is able to use it even in the insignificant lines, the casually dropped conversational digressions.

She makes her début in her seventeenth year. Her appearance is naturally a triumph; and in that instant her existence is transformed into a matter of national concern. Just as the daughter of the regiment[12] is regarded as a daughter by the whole regiment, so she becomes the nation's daughter. The very first sight of her is enough to convince everyone that it would be difficult to find more than one woman in a generation who is so exceptionally and happily gifted. It therefore becomes a national duty to admire her and a common concern to preserve this rare flower. Furthermore, it must follow as a matter of course from human weakness that it becomes, if not quite a duty, at any rate a matter of inquisitive interest to see how long she will last. Yes, human rejoicing over the exception is strange; almost from the first and highest moment of rejoicing, inquisitiveness begins to plot the ambush. It is not envy, far from that, it is a kind of giddiness mingled in the admiration, which is beside itself for joy until it occurs to it already in the first year to develop this fatal tension, and out of pure admiration begins to admire in an almost suspicious way.

But let us recall what has already been suggested more than once: If there lived at the same time an essential aesthetician and he were called upon to attempt critically to evaluate this actress or one of her performances, he would certainly say: No, her time has not yet really come.

III

Fourteen years pass, and she is in her thirty-first year. Through all these years she has received constant recognition and admiration. Permit me to indicate this passing of time by using the interval to offer some observations. For let us not be deceived by a careless calculation of all her apparent privileges, and thereby be led unfairly to envy her this admiration. Let us rather consider how much blockheadedness is mixed into the constant mauling of this trivial recognition; and above all let us not forget what it signifies that during these fourteen years it has actually become a habit of her contemporaries to admire her; if we wish to consider the matter correctly, let us not be so unfair to her as to forget to subtract this factor from the supposed splendour of the admiration. Oh, how seldom is there found a person, let alone an age, that does not yield to the fraud of habit; so that even if the expression is not changed, this unchanged expression still becomes something different through force of habit; so that what is literally the same nevertheless sounds so weak, so mechanical, so toneless, even though the same thing is said. Oh, much is said in the world about seducers and seduction: but how many are there who do not deceive themselves through habit, so that they seem unchanged but actually are wasting away in the inner man; so that they still love the same people, love them, but so tamely, so shabbily; so that they still use the same tender expressions, but so feebly, so mechanically, so lifelessly. Suppose a king decided to visit a humble family – yes, the family would feel honoured, proud, almost overwhelmed by its good fortune. But suppose His Majesty should decide to continue visiting the same family every day. How long would it be before the king must almost make an effort to give a little significance to the fact that he is visiting the family? While the family would remain unchanged, and from habit would continue to say: we thank you for the great honour. Of all sophists, time is the most dangerous, and of all dangerous sophists, habit is the most crafty. It is already difficult enough to notice that one is changed little by little over the years. But the fraud of habit is that one remains unchanged, that one says the same thing, while in fact he is utterly changed and says it in an utterly different way.

Just for that reason, all those who in truth serve the truth uselessly, that is, without putting it to selfish uses, for whom life is a sheer struggle with the sophisms of existence, whose concern is not how they can best profit for themselves, but how they can most truly serve the truth and in truth benefit mankind: such persons have been well-informed about the use of deceptions – in order to test mankind.[13] For example, when an outstanding man lives in deep seclusion, when he only rarely shows himself, then people are not spoiled by too much exposure to him. On the contrary, there develops a splendid, and, if you will, an expedient deception: that this excellent man must really be something quite extraordinary. And why? Because people know how to value his splendid qualities? Oh, no – because they see him so rarely that this rare appearance produces a fantastic effect. Ample experience from the past shows that this can be done. The method, masterfully expressed by Shakespeare in Henry IV's address to Prince Henry,[14] has been used successfully by a numerous host of kings and emperors and clerics and Jesuits and diplomats and shrewd pates, etc. Among them have probably been many superior persons, quite a number of whom have also wished to serve the truth, but all of them were nevertheless united in wishing to operate with the aid of a deception. Either they have simply sought to benefit themselves by arousing the awe of the masses, or they have perhaps piously but also shrewdly hoped to put the truth into general circulation with the aid of – a deception. The absolutely unselfish servants of the truth, on the other hand, have always followed the practice of moving about among people a great deal. They have never played hide and seek with the masses in order again to play the game of bedazzlement by exhibiting themselves on rare occasions as the objects of stunned amazement. They have on the contrary always shown themselves regularly, in everyday clothes, lived with the common man, chatted in the streets and byways, and renounced all prestige – for when the masses see a man every day, they think to themselves: Is that all? Oh well, '*mundus vult decipi*'. But the disinterested witnesses to the truth have never wished to join in this deception, they have never been willing to meet the masses half-way by adding the rest: '*decipiatur ergo*'.[15] They have on the contrary deceived in the opposite way, that is, they have passed judgement on the world by seeming insignificant.

Suppose that an author who neither has a significant fund of ideas nor is very hard-working should once in a great while publish a decorative copybook, very dainty and elegantly put together, with many blank pages: then the masses would look upon this decorative phenomenon with wonder and admiration. They would think: since it has taken him so long to write it, and since there is so little written on the pages, it must be something really extraordinary. Suppose on the other hand that a highly productive author, who has other things to think about than being decorative and profiting from a deception, should by exerting himself with greater and greater diligence find himself able to work with exceptional speed. The masses would soon get used to that, and would think: it must be a careless job.[16] For of course the masses cannot judge whether something is really worked out or not, so they stick to – the deception. Suppose there were a pastor, who like the late Chaplain-to-the-Court in Berlin, the otherwise so highly-gifted Theremin[17] preached only every eighth Sunday or even just every twelfth, but who did so in the most regal and

exalted presence of Their Majesties and the whole royal household: a deception would therefore immediately develop about
such a Head-Chaplain-to-the-Court. He becomes – well, in
truth he of course remains what he really is, a highly gifted
man. But in the eyes of the masses he becomes not only the
Head-Chaplain-to-the-Court but a Right Reverend Sir besides, or a Right Ruffled Head-Chaplain-to-the-Court, something Right Resplendent, like the king's golden coach, which
one beholds with awe only a few times a year. The masses will
be deeply impressed, and in their wisdom they will reflect as
follows: such a preacher needs three months just to prepare
one sermon and memorize it, so it must be extraordinary. And
behold, the crowd of curiosity-seekers is so great on the long-
awaited eighth or twelfth Sunday that the Head-Chaplain-to-
the-Court is scarcely able to squeeze up into the pulpit – had
he preached only once a year, the crowd would have been so
huge that he would not have been able to squeeze down again
at all, or policemen and armed sextons would have been
needed to secure the Right Reverend Head-Chaplain's going
out and coming in.[18] And if the crowd were so great that
someone were squeezed and trampled to death, then the next
time the crowd would be still greater. For the dictum holds
with regard not only to the truth, but also to curiosity:
'Sanguis martyrum est semen ecclesiae.' [19]

And now an actress, who for fourteen years has been a
constant object of admiration. One has seen her many times,
and has slept on one's admiration. One knows perfectly well
that she is staying in the country. If only she were one of those
personages who travel around Europe, then she could still
hope for the assistance of the deception. But one knows that
she must remain in the city, because in Denmark there is only
one city and one theatre; indeed, one knows that she must
play, because she is engaged to do so. Despite their admiration, many are perhaps even shameless enough to be quite
aware that she *must* play, because that is the way she earns

her living; one knows perfectly well that one can get to see her, generally twice a week. Granted that one continues constantly to admire; but how many are there in a generation who know how to preserve their fervour and discrimination with such vigilance that in their admiration's fourteenth year they can view her with the same originality, with the same freshness that she preserves! No, mankind is similar also in this respect to the children in the market place.[20] When they realize that they possess something, that they are allowed to keep it, then they become ungrateful, or if not downright ungrateful then at least sluggish from the habit of admiration. Towards no one is mankind therefore so ungrateful as it is towards God, just because people have the sluggish notion that one can always have Him – why, He cannot even die some day, to let people feel what they have lost. O human admiration, you are nothing but vanity, and not the least so when you mean to remain constant!

There has been no change in the expression of admiration and recognition, except in its intonation. The *spiritus asper*[21] of the first impression has slackened into the 'smooth breathing' of a vain, habitual admiration. The actress's stock stands unchanged at the quoted price, yet not quite so firm; a sneaking, anxious, basically well-meaning but in its inquisitiveness still treacherous reflection begins to mutter that she is getting older. No one wishes to admit it, and yet it is said, and yet no one wishes to admit having said it. The tension of the embarrassment is all the more painful, just because her existence has been a matter of national concern. People mean well so far as she is concerned (for we will not dwell here on the part that somebody's envy can play in the origin of such an opinion); they are really indignant against time for making her older, having once settled themselves comfortably in the habit of an admiration that would make her remain eighteen years old for ever. Nobody considers how ungrateful it is to make her metamorphosis more and more difficult, how ungratefully she is served when fond memory is transformed into opposition at the critical moment; and nobody considers that this whole thing is a galimatias, which has no place at all, especially in aesthetics, since only with the metamorphosis will her time really begin.

IV
(*Last Article*)

So now for the metamorphosis. This actress was constituted by feminine youthfulness, though not in the usual sense of the term. What is normally called youthfulness falls prey to the years; for the grip of time may be most loving and careful, but it seizes everything finite just the same. But in this actress there has been an essential genius which corresponds to the very idea: feminine youthfulness. This is an idea, and an idea is something quite different from the phenomenon of being seventeen years old. A girl, after all, can be utterly devoid of any idea and still be seventeen years old. Without this correspondence of genius to an idea there could be no talk of a metamorphosis. But just because this is the case, and the idea is what it is without compromise, the metamorphosis is exceptional. Just as nature preserves its continuity by means of anticipation and recollection, foresight and hindsight, which naturalists have felicitously termed the Promethean and the Epimethean:[22] so in the spiritual realm that which is to constitute the metamorphosis must be present from the beginning, but only after some time has passed can it be brought decisively into play or decisively manifest itself. Its manifestation is precisely the metamorphosis.

A woman who only possesses feminine youthfulness in the ordinary sense cannot receive the metamorphosis, since feminine youthfulness in this sense is not dialectical within itself. It has only a single life, which is simply consumed by the entrance of the dialectical rather than being set apart and singled out. Time is the dialectical which comes from without,[23] which therefore consumes this undialectical youth-fulness sooner or later. But suppose youthfulness is also alive in another dimension; then in destroying something of the natural youthfulness time simply makes the genius more manifest, and manifest in ideality's pure aesthetic relation to the idea. The actress will of course not become young again in the ridiculous sense, according to which butchers' apprentices and the public speak of a devilishly lively girl, but only in the sense of ideality will she become young or younger. She is now really a proper subject for an essential critique, now that she comes into relation to the same idea for the second time and raised to the second power; or more precisely expressed, precisely because it is the second time does she came to relate herself to the idea in a purely ideal way. The matter is quite simple. One might ask: which medium corresponds essen-tially to a genius whose idea is feminine youthfulness? Most people would presumably give the worst answer: it is feminine youthfulness itself, or being seventeen years old. But this is certainly a misunderstanding which conflicts with the dialectic's own movement of thought. The purely ideal and dialectical requirement is that the medium, or that in which the idea exists, is related to the idea at a distance from the idea. With respect to all natural characteristics it holds true that the first time is the highest, is the culmination. But it holds with respect to ideality that the second time is the highest; for what is ideality but precisely: the second time. From the standpoint of ideality, the fact of being quite young is not appropriate at all to the embodiment of the idea of youthfulness in a role. Unaesthetic spectators think otherwise because they suffer under a delusion; they confuse their enjoy-ment of Miss N. N.'s phenomenal youthfulness with an appre-ciation of the actress's essential ideality. Let us take another example. There is a form of lyricism which one may call the lyricism of youthfulness. Every young person who is *erectioris ingenii*[24] has a little of it. But then there is a young person, who *qua* youth has this lyricism of youthfulness, and also possesses a genius the idea of which is the lyricism of youthfulness. Now let us ask, when will he produce his best lyrics, in his twentieth year do you suppose? By no means. His best lyrics will come just at some more mature age when time has taken away the happy accidents of his youthfulness, so that he will now relate himself to his idea in a purely ideal way, and thereby also in a deeper sense as its *servant*. Those who only have a taste for the happy accidents of his early youth are lacking in aesthetic cultivation, and therefore do not discover that these delights belong to the accidental, the transitory, while the genius and the relation to the idea are the eternal and the essential.

The most demanding role which can be assigned an actress who embodies the idea of feminine youthfulness in its most lyrical potentiation is certainly that of Juliet in *Romeo and Juliet*. I wonder whether it would really occur to an aesthetician that a seventeen-year-old actress could play Juliet? There is indeed much trumpeting about the complete play of powers, the fire, the ardour, and many other things of that sort, but these things are really spoken of in gallery-categories, which are hardly sufficient for judging an interpretation of Juliet. What the gallery wishes to see is of course not an ideal presentation, a portrayal of the ideal. The gallery wishes to see Miss Juliet, a devilishly pretty and damn lively girl of eighteen years, who plays at Juliet or passes herself off as Juliet, while the gallery is diverted by the thought that it is really Miss N. N. Therefore the gallery can naturally never get into its head that precisely in order to *portray* Juliet it is essential that an actress possess a distance in age from Juliet. And yet it is so, and that admired excess of powers in the eighteenth year is really, aesthetically, a misunderstanding. For in ideality it holds true that the prime power is consciousness and transparency, which knows how to be in control of the essential powers, in the service, be it well noted, of an idea.

There certainly are roles in which the eighteen years are *quod desideratur*[25] in an actress, but these roles are simply not the eminently demanding ones. There are roles in which this excess of powers which goes with the first youthfulness can be used as in a delightful game. Our actress may indeed undertake these roles, and the undertaking can be regarded as a lovely and also worthwhile way of passing the time until she becomes mature enough to acquire the necessary powers for sustaining the eminent assignments. To portray a little maiden of sixteen years in a French play would be a suitable role. But toying with this fleeting, teasing fragility is also to be considered as nothing compared with bearing the weight of Juliet's intensive fullness. It would of course be a misunderstanding to suppose that anyone who could once portray such an almost sketchy figure should therefore also be in a position eventually to undertake the eminent roles. No, far from it. But just for that reason it is the exception when a person who has trained herself in the light forms of fleeting fairy-tale creatures, absolutely happy and constantly fresh and rejuvenated, should in the fullness of time be transfigured into the eminent hypostatis.

The metamorphosis will be a return, in the eminent sense, to her first condition. This will now be elucidated more precisely by exhibiting the dialectical determinants in the metamorphosis. As we have said, time is the dialectical that comes from without, but she was originally dialectical within herself. Just for that reason she can stand in opposition to time, so that its dialectic only makes manifest the dialectical in her – in the metamorphosis.

Time has asserted its right; it has taken something away from her immediate, her first, direct, fortuitous youthfulness. But again, in so doing time simply makes her genius the more essentially manifest. She has lost in the eyes of the gallery, she has won in the ideal sense. The time of gallery-confusions is past; if she is to play Juliet, there can no longer be any talk of creating a furore as Miss Juliet. If she is to play Juliet, it must be an eminent presentation, or more correctly a presentation in the eminent sense. And this is just the metamorphosis. Might against might, it is said, and so also here: dialectic against dialectic, so that time has no power really to take away, but only a subservient power, which serves to make manifest.

Time has asserted its right; it has taken something away from the lucky accidents or accidental luck of that first youthfulness. But it has also developed her, cultivating and refining her, so that now, in full and conscious, well-earned and dedicated command over her essential powers, she can in truth be the handmaiden of her idea. This is the essential aesthetic relation, and it is essentially different from the seventeen-year-old's immediate relation to her own youthfulness. It is this subservient relation to the idea which really is the culmination, precisely this conscious self-abnegation under the idea is the expression for the eminent elevation of her presentation. The youthfulness of the seventeenth year is much too fastidious, much too arrogant, much too lucky to serve in the deepest or (which is the same) in the highest sense. But to be entirely subservient is real inwardness. The inwardness of the seventeenth year is essentially an aspiration directed outward, which for all its luck can never be secure against one or another accident; even if the accident can be avoided, still it is a constant possibility, so that one must say each time: that was a stroke of luck. Only in the absolutely subservient relation to the idea is the accident made absolutely impossible.

Time has asserted its right; there is something which has been consigned to the past. But then again an ideality of recollection will cast an illumination of the highest sort over the whole presentation, an incarnation that was not present in those days of the first youthfulness. Only in recollection is there absolute rest, and therefore the still fire of the eternal, its incorruptible glow. And she is soothed in the eternity of her essential genius. She will not childishly or sadly long for the blaze of times past, for precisely in the metamorphosis has she become both too warm and too rich for that. This pure, soothing and rejuvenating recollection, as an idealizing light, will permeate the whole presentation, which in this light will become completely transparent.

Such are the moments of this metamorphosis. In order once again to illuminate its characteristic quality from another side, let us now in conclusion juxtapose another kind of metamorphosis for purposes of comparison. We shall choose one which is qualitatively different; this will give the comparison an essential interest, meanwhile forestalling any inquisitive quantifying as to which is the rarest, etc. This other metamorphosis is one of continuity, which again more closely defined is a process, a succession, a steady transformation through the years, such that the actress, as she grows older, gradually shifts her field and assumes older roles, again with the same perfection with which in her earlier years she filled the younger. One could call this metamorphosis the direct perfectibility. It has an especially ethical interest, and it will therefore be in the highest degree pleasing and convincing to a certain ethicist,[26] who in defence of his outlook on life proudly points to such a phenomenon as his triumph, and in quiet, intense gratitude regards such an actress as his almighty ally; for she proves his theory better than he, and at precisely one of its most perilous points. On the other hand, the metamorphosis of which we have spoken is one of potentiation, or a more and more intensive return to the original condition. This metamorphosis will be of absolute concern to an aesthetician, because the dialectic of potentiation is precisely the aesthetic-metaphysical dialectic. More joyfully than Archimedes will he utter the dithyrambic cry, 'Eureka!'[27] as he points to this phenomenon. Drunk with admiration and yet sober in dialectical self-possession, he will only have eyes for this single one, and will understand it as his mission to create a situation in which this marvel can be seen and admired just as such.

The metamorphosis of continuity will in the course of the

years extend itself uniformly over the essential range of roles included within the idea of feminity; that of potentiation will in the course of the years relate itself more and more intensively to the same idea, which, note well, is aesthetically understood the idea of femininity *sensu eminentissimo*. If one wishes to say of the actress who represents the metamorphosis of continuity that although she does not become older from the standpoint of temporality, she does become older from the standpoint of ideality, so one may say of the other that she becomes younger. But of both it may be said that time has no power over them. That is, there is one resistance against the power of the years, and that is perfectibility, which unfolds itself through the years; and there is another resistance to the power of the years, and that is potentiation, which precisely becomes manifest through the years. Both phenomena are essentially exceptions, and both have it in common that they become more exceptional with every year. Just because they are dialectically complex, their existence will also remain dialectical year after year. Each year will make the attempt to prove its thesis concerning the power of the years, but perfectibility and potentiation will triumphantly refute the years' thesis. This provides absolute tranquillity in the spectator, for the youthfulness of the seventeenth year is indeed fragile, but perfectibility and potentiation are absolutely dependable.

I hope this little article has succeeded in showing just how secure the essential actress's future really is, despite the years. If so it would be a fond satisfaction to me, so much the more because I am convinced that instead of the right conception of an actress's future there is manifold misunderstanding. For the same misunderstanding which misconstrues and unaesthetically overvalues the beginning also misconstrues and unaesthetically distorts what comes later, that is, the highest of all.

Summer 1847[28]

Inter et Inter

A PASSING COMMENT
ON A DETAIL IN DON JUAN

by A[1]

published in two parts
in *The Fatherland*
May 19–20, 1845

A PASSING COMMENT ON A DETAIL IN DON JUAN

Mozart's *Don Juan*[2] has again been brought to the stage. By comparison with a good deal of its other warmed-over fare, delicate but unnourishing, the theatre has in this opera what the cook might call a well-spiced tidbit; one can get the good out of it for a long time. Even though it is seldom performed the public is pleased enough to see that it can be given at all. The newspapers have already issued their decrees regarding the performance as a whole and in its details, but I do not presume to have an opinion quite so quickly, not even about the evaluation-business carried on by the newspapers. The late Socrates had a fine old rule that one might draw modest conclusions from the little bit one understands about a thing to the large amount that one does not understand;[3] the theatre criticism in the newspapers always inclines me to an extreme modesty and an ascetic restraint from any conclusion.

Much has been said regarding Herr Hansen's performance,[4] pronounced in all-inclusive terms yet infallibly and with an admirable readiness, which is ready at once. I cannot presume to have any such sweeping judgement ready at once. On the other hand there is a single point which caught my attention and on which I should like to dwell for a moment, if I may solicit the interest of a reader; for I do not wish to detain anyone who is in a hurry, or to waste the time of busy shopkeepers. I dwell upon this detail all the more readily since I look upon it, not as the climax of Hr. H.'s total conception and rendition, on which I have in general no opinion, but as a splendid moment nevertheless, whether this actor has performed just as well throughout (which indeed cannot cloud the brilliance of a single detail) or has not performed as well at other points (which could only make this brilliant scene more conspicuous by comparison). This point is the duet with Zerlina in the first act,[5] which must be seen as an absolute triumph, whatever one may otherwise think of the value of recitatives for performance on our stage.

Not only is a superior voice required of a singer, but also a good delivery, which is the unity of voice and mood, something different than the voice's flexibility in executing coloratura passages and runs. For potentially there is the mutual commensurability, and in actual execution the consonance of voice and mood in the delivery; finally, it is required of the dramatic singer that the mood be correct in relation to situation and poetic individuality. When the singer has a voice and applies mood to it then he is artistically in passion; if he is also an actor, he will even be able through facial expression to hold contradictory elements together at the same time. The more reflective he himself is, and skilled in letting the voice play on the pianoforte of moods, the more combinations he will have at his disposal, and so be able most completely to fulfil the composer's demands, assuming that the composer's work is of the sort that does make demands on the singer's performance, and does not belong to the class of operas that can be neither performed nor endured. If he is less reflective, he will not have so great a range in mood and character. But he must still have one thing: the universal ground of all mood, the ability to apply imagination to the voice, the ability to sing with imagination. Such a delivery is what I have admired in Hr. H. at the point referred to.

One necessarily expects a great deal from the duet with Zerlina. The first scene with Anna[6] is too stormy to enable one to get a clear impression of Don Juan. But here everything is put in order, the setting has receded into the background, and attention is concentrated on how Don Juan will conduct himself the first time he really springs to the attack. One thinks: now we shall get to see whether Don Juan is a fop, a windbag (as a person becomes who tries to be a Don Juan), who has in Leporello a naïve trumpeter and in Mozart a feeble troubadour, or whether he is indeed that man of renown and the most famous work of that composer of renown.

The composer performs magnificently. The accompaniment is ingratiating and persuasive, it returns enchantingly, like the repeated murmur of a brook, as the orchestra looks after itself and continues on and on and cannot stop. It brings on dreaminess, but yet captivation, as the fragrance of flowers brings on anesthesia; it leads off into the infinite, not with the energy of passion but with a quiet yearning. Mozart knows well enough what he is doing, and a Zerlina is not meant to have the qualities of individuality which would be appropriate to a different conception, as for example the most powerful eruption of passion in a mutuality of desire, in which womanly craving is almost a match in energy and daring for Juan's force of nature; or a womanly abandonment to Juan, in which infinite womanly riches are given over; or a conquered resistance, still proud in its collapse; or a noble simplicity which is deceived; or an exalted purity which is defiled; or a humble sincerity which, violated once, is violated for a lifetime; or a deep trustfulness which, disappointed, is disappointed for ever; or the holy passion of the infinite which is led off into perdition; or womanly foolishness which is brought to ruin, etc. Zerlina's seduction is a quiet wedding, which is brought off without any great spectacle.

Essentially it comes about in this way: she didn't know how it happened, but yet it happened, and so she was seduced;* and the result of Zerlina's utmost exertion to comprehend the

---

* Therefore Leporello and Zerlina would be able to come to a splendid understanding were he to tell her regarding Don Juan what he said in the old days to Elvira, which upset her so much: 'Yes! oh, yes! it is most strange, for he is no sooner here than he is gone.'⁷ And so Zerlina would say: 'Yes, isn't that just how it is, I always say that one can't tell how it happens at all.'

matter is this: that one cannot explain it. This is of great importance in the interpretation of Zerlina. It was therefore an error for an otherwise laudable actress, Madame Kragh,[8] to sing the line, 'No! I will not,' with a strong emphasis, as though a decision were brewing in Zerlina. Far from it. She is befuddled, giddy in the head and with queer feelings around the heart, right from the beginning. If one puts thoughts in her head at this point, the whole opera has been misconstrued.* The line which follows: 'Masetto will be furious,' has the same force. If this is rendered in an earnestly sympathetic way, the whole thing is a failure. These lines must therefore not mean more and must not be sung otherwise than to stand *au niveau*[10] with involuntary gesticulations, such as clutching her apron, or wriggling out of Don Juan's embrace. This just makes her beautiful and lovable, and her relation to Masetto correct. It is a sheer misunderstanding to hear the aria, *'Batti, batti'*,[11] as an act of reconciliation with Masetto. She still does not entirely have her wits about her; meagre as they are, they are always more than sufficient to cope with

---

* In that case the whole design is altered: i.e. the profound and Greek touch, that Don Juan should trip over a straw, over a little Zerlina, while he is actually falling before quite other powers.[9] The total effect and the unity of the whole would be destroyed. Anna's passion, the murder of the Commandant, the meeting with Elvira, everything goes against Don Juan; he is almost brought to a standstill, and for the first time in his life he is gasping for breath. All this is brought about so early, in the first two scenes, that the opera is still just beginning. What sort of seduction shall this be now, which takes place during the opera? One of two sorts: either one which is so difficult and perilous that the strain will excite his uttermost passion and uttermost strength (which of course will weaken the effect and be weakened by the effect of Anna and Elvira); or that of an insignificant, lovable little peasant girl, childlike and naturally playful, roguish, a feminine type to which only approximations are found in the North, and for which the Catholic Church has a mixed category. Don Juan is in his element, but the effect of the others in the opera is not weakened. This is Mozart's intention, and in this intention the opera has its beautiful unity and Mozart his happy task. Don Juan and Zerlina are in an immediate relation to one another, as a force of nature to its natural purpose, a pure musical relation.

Masetto's domestic arrangements, though not with Don Juan's snare. She sees that Masetto is angry, so there is nothing to do but straighten the matter out with him, for her own sake. For the whole affair has remained unclear to her, and in her innocence she has never doubted her innocence. She must be conceived in this naïveté; she really cannot understand what is wrong with Masetto, that he can be so angry. Hence the reconciliation must not bear a serious character here, as though she were now saved. By no means; for as soon as she sees Don Juan it all begins again, and so she must go again and coax Masetto a little, and so she comforts him, and so she herself believes in the end that Don Juan and Masetto are just being quarrelsome with each other, God knows why, and it is up to her to talk them into a reasonable frame of mind. Let a few years pass, and then go and visit Madame Masetto; you will find Zerlina essentially unchanged. Just as she goes and plays about in the opera, so now she goes and bustles about in his house, pretty, sweet as can be, etc. If you should ask her, 'But what about this business, now, with that fellow Don Juan?' she would reply, 'Goodness, that was strange, a strange wedding day, such a hullabaloo, and I had to be running about everywhere; one moment it was Masetto growling around, then Don Juan wanting to chat with me, and if I hadn't been there, sure as anything they would have killed each other.'

She must be conceived in this way, in order to be clear about her difference as a woman from Anna and Elvira. Anna is by comparison far less guilty than Zerlina. She has confused Juan with Octavio, nothing more. But because she is essentially developed, that is enough to upset her deeply, perhaps for the rest of her life. She conceals it so long as possible, and then she rages for revenge.[12] But Zerlina has no regrets, and goes blithely on her way both to the dance with Don Juan and to confession with Masetto; it is all some odd something-or-other, and each of her honourable partners seems all right at the time. She comes along everywhere, she feels that she is in company with the well-born ladies and is just as important as some of the others. She takes part in capturing Don Juan, not because he has seduced her, but because he has hurt Masetto (it is clear that she confounds the physical and the moral), and she therefore finds Leporello to be just as guilty, because he has also abused Masetto, her own little Masetto of whom she is so fond and whom the others have treated so badly.[13]

Elvira is a tremendous feminine figure, in that she comprehends with absolute passion what it means to be seduced. She does not wish simply to save a little bit of her honour, but to bring Don Juan to a halt, naturally with the reservation that if Don Juan will be faithful to her she will give up her wandering mission – but in that case he would also be brought to a halt. That is authentically feminine, a superb invention. Yet she is in a way *ausser sich*[14] in her mission, considered as a woman, and therefore must necessarily be cast in a comic light. I am not referring to that deeply tragic situation in the second act where she takes Leporello for Don Juan,[15] of which an author has said that it is almost gruesome,[16] but to something else. She herself has been seduced, and now she wishes to save someone else, without considering that such an undertaking requires preparation and much consideration, in order to acquire the ability to put oneself in the other's place. She simply cannot do that. Therefore she is quite unable to make herself understandable to Zerlina. Here Elvira becomes comic. She transfers her whole pathos to Zerlina,[17] and in the end Zerlina can better understand Don Juan than comprehend Elvira. An actress who portrays Zerlina dares not, therefore, as the opera was performed in the old days, become terrified, gripped by anxiety at Elvira's story; that is much too much. She should be amazed at this new surprise, and amazed in such a way that a good spectator almost smiles at the situation, even while he grasps the tragic in Elvira.

(concluded tomorrow)

II
(*Conclusion*)

Now for Don Juan. Suppose the singer applies imagination to the voice and uses this delivery as a kind of an accompaniment, what then? Then the situation becomes one of seduction? Perhaps, but not in an opera. In a drama, on the contrary, in which a seducer sings not *to* the girl but *for* the girl, he can help in this way to bring her into a state of phantasy. I shall sketch such a situation. Suppose we have to do, not with a peasant girl, but with a Donna, a developed young lady with significant qualities. The seducer has a voice, and he knows how to apply imagination to it. So he sometimes sings to her whatever she would like to hear. Then one day he chooses by accident, so it is said, this song from *Don Juan*. He delivers it with the full strength of an inspired imagination. He naturally does not look at her; not a glance, not a suggestion of desire, or all is lost. He gazes off into space, and his voice is transmuted into the mood and phantasy of enticement. So the Donna listens, secure as she is, and since she knows that he is not singing *to* her, that it has nothing to do with her, she gives herself over to infatuation. Since they are assumed to be equal in power, the seducer must create the first rendezvous in phantasy, face to face only in the rarefied medium of imaginative intuition and presentiment. Even if this situation should be presented it would still not be essentially an opera, though in a drama or narrative the transition could be constructed from this phantasy-situation to the reflected reality of the seduction.[18]

Now if it were Herr Hansen's task to create this situation in a drama one may be sure that his delivery would be *omnibus numeris absoluta*,[19] and certainly no one who has a sense for observations of this sort will deny that it is striking to hear such an excellent delivery. Calm, with insinuations in the voice, dreamy and full of longing yet distinct in expression, articulating every note so that nothing is wasted or goes to waste, he would produce a rare effect. But when we have to do with an opera – and that is our concern here – then this excellent delivery is not 'a golden apple in a silver bowl,'[20] but quite out of place. Don Juan is no amorous zither-strummer, nor a seducer either, of the sort who might use such a disguise to make his first onslaught.[21] Let us take another passage in the opera, the guitar-aria[22] for example, or the point at which Don Juan joins in (*'poverina, poverina'*) with Elvira's opening aria.[23] I should say, dwelling on the latter, that here this delivery ought to be used. This outburst is essentially directed to no one. Don Juan stands, as it were, taking counsel with himself and anticipating some pleasure. Therefore imagination should be applied to the voice, and the ironical must not appear in Don Juan's reflection on the situation, but must be left to the spectator, who understands Don Juan. The actor ought therefore to take care that he be at rest at that instant, though it is otherwise correct that he should pace to and fro in a certain tension during the aria. But above all, he must not step forward when he sings these words, because Elvira is not supposed to hear them. Nor should they be sung to Leporello, as are the rest of his lines during the aria. Essentially they mean only that Don Juan is in humour. The matchless effect of the situation must not result from Don Juan's reflection or calculation, but is to be sought in the effect of the whole, as an author has pointed out.[24]

In the duet with Zerlina, Don Juan sings *to* Zerlina. This is *Don Juan*, and Zerlina is a dear little peasant girl. In relation to that Donna in the situation we invented it was necessary to begin as we suggested, because there was no question of making demands on her at once. Therefore it began with an innocent daydream. And with all seduction the rule holds: an abortive attack, and all is lost. Just because Zerlina is a peasant girl, it does not therefore follow that Don Juan should begin with some stroke of impudence; Don Juan never does that. Not self-consciously, but like a force of nature, he always possesses dignity and grace. The recitatives before the duet are even languishing, in a good sense. That is quite correct, because Don Juan is without reflection. Anyway, to project a peasant girl into some sort of vast fantasy decked out in a mantle of idealization, when someone like Don Juan knows perfectly well that she already has enough to do just gazing upon and adoring the beautiful man, would be just the thing to make her befuddled in the head. To be sure, a fellow over hasty in forcing an embrace would be only too quickly understood by Zerlina and would put her on her guard, for in all her naïveté Zerlina is modest and won't put up with any nonsense; but the fantasy she would not understand at all. At the same time, and as an absolutely decisive key to the text, one needs to see how fully in command Don Juan is, to see him catch the fly with sweets, to see that he is right in a certain sense when he tells Elvira (of his affair with Zerlina), 'that was only a little diversion'.[25] This line is not malicious, nor is it ironical; it is the simple truth. Don Juan considers Elvira to be too magnificent to be affected by a little liaison with a little Zerlina. She the seduced woman $\kappa\alpha\tau'\dot{\epsilon}\xi o\chi\dot{\eta}\nu$,[26] and Zerlina! It would be easy enough to endow Don Juan with a little reflection, but in the opera the art is precisely to avoid doing so, so that Don Juan shall not, through a little reflection, become a humdrum figure and the opera be fatally flawed in construction. By means of attitude, expression, gesture, representation, with the whole authentic force of the character, the actor must achieve overwhelming command.

So the duet begins. The dreamy universality of the accompaniment (music being a more universal medium)[27] must be clearly audible when Don Juan applies himself to seize Zerlina through the force of nature which is in both himself and the accompaniment. When at the climactic moment he sees her confusion, and sees that her resistance is only a veiled submission, he summons his whole power of command into an

almost irresistible control. He has the self-confidence of a
natural power. The accompaniment for the first, 'Be mine!' is
therefore not ingratiating, but energetic and decisive. Now she
gives in. For Don Juan it is naturally different. Here again
one must see his overwhelming command. In relation to such
as Anna and Elvira it is not inconceivable that in the moment
of his triumph Don Juan should enjoy such a strong delight
that he is first like a lover, who gives just as much as he takes,
and then only in the next moment is a seducer. But Zerlina is
captivated and served in a different way. Here the enjoyment
lies precisely in the amusing diversion, and Don Juan is in an
immediate, purely musical sense in his element. Zerlina is not
for him at all inferior to any other woman, but something
different than Elvira or Anna, and one who in her own way is
just as desirable and engages him essentially just as much. I
wish to repeat, therefore, that Zerlina must be conceived in
such a way that when she is seen and heard in relation to Don
Juan she will produce in a good spectator a certain exhilara-
tion, because it will be impossible for him to use the serious
category[28] against her, and when she is seen in relation to
Masetto she will elicit a smile. For Zerlina is essentially neither
seduced nor saved, but blown about constantly in the wind.[29]

It may be that one or another, or several, or even most
people will consider this whole article to be a trifle since, to
be sure, one almost never sees Zerlina made the subject of an
aesthetic interpretation. I am myself inclined to view it as a
trifle, and feel therefore obliged to beg Herr Hansen's pardon
in case, seeing his name being used, he should perhaps put
himself to the trouble of reading this piece; and also to ask
The Fatherland's forgiveness, since I have, curiously enough,
burdened its pages with such a study, the deficiency of which
is precisely that it is not weighty enough. Herr Hansen can
easily afford to forgive me. What luck, when a man aspires to
something and makes his choice in life, then to have the kind
of singing voice that he has; what luck, when a man has an

aspiration and has chosen his vocation as an actor, then to have so many good qualifications as he really has. When a man has been given so much, and has acquired a good deal besides, he can easily afford to waste a little practice-time on his gait and posture. Far be it from me to imagine that my legs or my gait bear any relation to my conception of this most immortal opera; I ought to be looking soon for other legs to walk on.[30]

in the comic opera *Ludovic*
A Recollection Offered in Remembrance

by *Procul*[1]

HERR PHISTER AS CAPTAIN SCIPIO

(in the comic opera *Ludovic*)

A Recollection Offered in Remembrance

It may seem haphazard and odd to discuss just one particular role portrayed by such a wide-ranging artist as Herr
Phister, and if one must discuss a single portrayal then it
again seems haphazard and odd to choose just Captain Scipio.
Well, this choice is indeed haphazard or there is something
haphazard in it; so it is, and so be it. Least of all is there
any drivel implied to the effect that this role is the best, the
nicest, etc. No, there is something haphazard about this choice.
The point is that 'Captain Scipio' is an eminent portrayal in
that mode which is Phister's forte: reflection. To that extent
it is essentially correct to make it a subject of a critique. It is
characteristic of a critique which deals with reflection that it
gets down to the particular, delves into the particular, and to
that extent it is essentially correct as regards Herr Phister –
instead of indulging in generalities which cannot say much in
this case – to make a particular portrayal the subject of a
detailed critique. The haphazard feature is that this portrayal
in particular has happened to appeal to the author. But there
is some such happenstance involved in all true infatuation.
The girl in love certainly owns many other and far more costly
dresses than that one with the blue stripes or the red trim that
she was wearing when her lover first saw her; and yet this
dress possesses a special value for him. When his sweetheart
dresses up to go with him to a party, hence dresses for others
– yes, then she is adorned in silks, etc.; but when she really
dresses up, that is, only for him, then she puts this dress on.

So also here. And in truth, however abundantly the richest
young girl may be endowed so far as dresses are concerned,

she will still scarcely be so richly endowed as Herr Phister's repertoire is, with the most varied and sumptuous costumes. But one of them has for one spectator a purely accidental value, another for another. That is, it is as though he were infatuated with it, and when he has to speak, he prefers to choose this one to speak about; or rather, not 'when he has to speak', since it is a joy, a delight, a satisfaction for him to speak of it. In this way, in fact, he may come gradually to understand that all infatuation is really basically self-love;[2] for there is indeed some self-love involved in the wish to have understood a masterful portrayal completely, or even in a completely different way than others, and approximately as the artist has himself.

First, just a few general observations. Herr Phister's forte is: *reflection*. There is therefore scarcely any actor on the stage so *diligent* as he, and not very many who have a notion of what *diligence* is. Diligence is here to be taken in the pregnant sense: *study*, thoughtfulness, reflective attention to every detail, even the least. Of course it is said in general of every actor that he does some studying; one sometimes hears complaints that someone has not studied his role, or an actor sometimes even offers the excuse that he has not had time to study his role sufficiently. But how many are there actually who are able to study a role, who have an artistically developed concept of what it means to study a role? Most actors study the way Trop 'stoddies',[3] and it is therefore thoughtless to accuse them of not studying their roles on some particular occasion; and it is a no less queer manner of talking when they themselves sometimes complain that they have not had time to study. For just from Trop's example it can be seen that the length of time is after all not quite the decisive factor in the matter of 'studying'. It is otherwise with Herr Phister. Even if there is sometimes only a very short time for studying a role, essentially one can still see the results of study in his performance. For 'study' is exactly Herr Phister's essential strength. He can devote the longest time to a study, but he can use even the shortest time in such an intensively thoughtful way that it becomes study. Therefore there is perhaps hardly another actor on our stage who feels, to the degree he does, the burden of carrying out any particular portrayal, just because he has so little immediacy and so much reflection, that is, just because every single portrayal is in the strictest sense a study, is a totality thoroughly reflected upon in every minute detail.[4]

But for this reason there is also no other actor on our stage who has so much cause for complaint as Phister has against the wretched critic who has nothing but interjections to offer. Even a comedian in the immediate mode might well wish that the critic would act as an interpreter who would sometimes disclose whatever was to be found in his performance, since the artist himself is not conscious of it. But the performance of a reflective comedian, who is conscious of every insignificant minutia, constitutes a demand that he be given back again with the same precision what he has with such precision presented. The immediate genius has himself an affinity to the interjection; but reflection is by its own nature akin only to reflection, and must demand of the critic the trick, if you will, of being able to analyse another man's performance in all its details, to account for every detail, and then to put it together again as a whole. Herr Phister really suffers in this regard under the trifling habits of our situation. Any particular performance of his usually creates an obligation, but of such magnitude in the currency of reflection and consciousness, that the critics hereabouts seek to cash it in vain, or more likely do not even make the attempt; so he is, as an artist, in the situation of the Englishman living in a country town, who almost came into financial embarrassment because he owned a banknote that no one could change.

To respond to an act of reflection or a reflective performance by saying nothing more nor less than *'Bravo!'* or even *'Bravissimo!'* is utterly senseless. It is something that can only bore and weary the reflection which is the object of such admiration, and something that easily becomes an exchange like that which Poul Møller has recorded between a Japanese and a Danish sailor: The Japanese said, 'Tanko – Panko,' to which the sailor quite appropriately replied, 'Well blow me down.'[5] Admiration directed at reflection, must be expressed in the language of reflection, not that of immediacy. Reflection is this: Why? – because .... Why is the whole thing constructed in this way? – because .... Why is this little stroke here – it is because, etc. Everything is consciousness. Again, to admire is to be able to discover and understand the whole: Why? – because ... True admiration in the relation between reflection and reflection (and only like understands like) is therefore complete understanding, neither more nor less. In a certain sense, there is therefore no admiration in the relation between reflection and reflection. If reflection A is the performer, and reflection B approaches to admire, what does that mean? It means that B seeks to show that he has understood A completely. If he has succeeded, then A replies, 'Yes, so it is. I know that perfectly well myself.' If there is to be any talk of admiration, it could arise just as properly over the fact that reflection B so perfectly understands A. But this also cancels out; for B will have to reply, 'Yes, so it is. I know that perfectly well myself.' That is to say, understanding between reflection and reflection is quits. There remains no incommensurability, the account balances, and just from this fact arises the infinite distance of ideality between reflection and reflection.

Such distance is the true relation between reflection and reflection. People who possess a little reflection do not realize this. They have lost immediacy's beautiful passion for admiration. Their scrap of reflection hence develops a certain inhibition in them; this is what becomes critical pettiness and envy.

But such is not the case where the admiring reflection is essentially reflective; there the relationship is correct between the admiring reflection and the reflection which is its object. There remains nothing of that critical pettiness, but also none of the pathology of immediate admiration, no palpitation, no congestion of the blood; in this relationship people do not clasp hands with each other, nor gaze in one another's eyes, there is no embracing, no falling on the knees, no arm in arm, no running together or curdling into *Gemütlichkeit*.[6] The relationship is as infinitely distant as possible, as aristocratically distant as mind can be from mind, and yet it is a relationship between admirers. This will seem to immediate enthusiasts to be the most inhuman thing imaginable. 'Two admirers,' they will say, 'and they do not instantly call each other by first names and drink together,' etc.? No, in the reflective relationship between reflection and reflection there is no place for first-name conviviality, there reigns only the most dignified use of polite address.

Ordinarily reviewers and other people prefer only to admire the immediate. The immediate, or immediate personalities, do not themselves know which end is up, what is good and what is poor. Furthermore, just because he has no self-consciousness, there is in the immediate personality a craving to hear this *Bravo, Bravissimo, schwere Noth, Gottes Blitz*! Here such admiration is quite unrestrained; if it makes a mistake and admires – a stupidity, something thoughtless, a blunder, etc., it doesn't matter. The one who is admired does not himself know which end is up, his game is blind man's buff, and besides it does him so much good to be admired. Under those circumstances it is easy enough to admire. It is otherwise with the reflective person and with a presentation which has been thoroughly thought through. The reflective performance is sheer consciousness; to admire is therefore in this case almost like submitting to an examination: whether one has understood or not, whether one knows anything or not. If one says something stupid here, no *Bravo* is any help, and a *Bravo* in the wrong place registers at once as a stupidity.

This consciousness is really the misfortune of every reflective presentation and of every highly reflective individual in relation to most people. This consciousness is what people call pride, ill nature, spite, irony – but immediacy's unconsciousness, which favours a quick and easy admiration, that is good nature, modesty, something lovable.

Scipio:
Captain in the Papal Police

The Papal Police is said to be distinguished by nothing much else than its brilliant uniform: almost full dress, with a bow and silver trim. According to what I have been told, it was Herr Phister's idea, when he undertook the role, to play it specifically in that costume; but this idea was rejected. I have heard further just why Herr Phister went on to insist on it emphatically; and the reason at once shows his reflection. Scipio is a man who is not exactly drunk, far from it, but who goes about even so in a perpetual state of tipsiness, perhaps because, as someone has written, it is more economical to sustain an inebriated condition day by day than to have to rise to it again and again. Now Herr Phister had rightly understood that drunkenness, half-drunkenness, or the slightly more elevated condition which one could call a diplomatic fogginess, would appear to the best advantage, that is, would be the more comical, the more brilliant the uniform is. That is quite right, for then the contradiction is greater. And the greater the opposition is between the drunken condition and the man's dignity, position in society, his dress or costume, or the greater the opposition is between his being drunk and the situation, the moment, the circumstances in which he is drunk: in short, the greater the contradiction, the more comical the drunkenness is. A police officer who is drunk is comic. But he is still more comic when in addition he is performing his

official function, and still more when for example his business
is to restore order in an ale-house where the people are utterly
drunk – and so is the police officer who in the name of public
authority orders them to disperse. And the comic stands out
all the stronger, the more brilliant his uniform is. The brilliant
uniform implies a claim, awakens an image – the drunkenness
completely shatters this by bringing out life's seamy side, by
turning it wrong side out. The more brilliant the outside of the
uniform is, the more shockingly the wrong side clashes with
it, and yet one sees both sides at once. For one sees the
brilliant uniform – and in addition that the man is drunk.

The idea was completely correct. But those who have not
seen Herr Phister's Scipio and only know this account of his
conception will be given an impression which does justice
neither to the presentation nor to Phister as a comedian. They
will almost be led to believe that Herr Phister has sacrificed
the role to the all too common conception of a military man in
gala uniform who is half drunk, a military man in full uniform
and 'full' in uniform.

But when one has seen and once again sees Herr Phister,
then he will correctly understand that this idea is merely
incidental to the whole conception, which lies much more
deeply and much more concretely in the comic.

What does it mean that Captain Scipio is a captain in the
Papal Police? It means that he is a man who wears a military
uniform, a man who marches at the head of soldiers, who
carries a gun, a man who reviews troops, a man who *qua*
military feels bound to military gallantry, to being charming
and almost dangerous where the fair sex is concerned. This
from the one side. But from the other side – and Captain
Scipio has two sides from which to be viewed; just in that fact
lies the more deeply comic, that Captain S. is an ambiguity.
From the other side, he is not really a military man at all, but
a captain in the police. From this side he is seen as something on the order of a justice of the peace, bailiff, fire

commissioner, street inspector, etc., in short, a civil servant. In fact, his official position is as remote as possible from any military situation. As a policeman he is perhaps in charge of keeping the gutters and sewers unclogged, he must apprehend drunks, keep an eye on the fish-wives, etc. etc.

What does this mean? It means that there is a contradiction here. Now there is no doubt that often, in real life, a well-bred person has been able to resolve such a contradiction and to develop an appealing character out of it. Nevertheless, it is certain that the contradiction is there; and it is also certain that when a true and reflective comedian seizes upon this contradiction, and knows how, convincingly but without exaggeration, to create a discord between these two persons in one (the soldier – and the civilian), then the comic effect is priceless.

This is in a deeper sense the comic in Captain Scipio, and is what Phister has splendidly understood, and therefore with fine comic art he makes use of slapstick, because he has not forgotten this contradiction either: the struggle to maintain his poise, in particular a posture in accord with his brilliant uniform, but all in vain, because he constantly has an extra incommensurable flourish, a little bit of the momentum which, to borrow a cabman's expression, can land a person in the gutter.

At any rate, Scipio is a military man. Not much needs to be done in this respect, since it is established by the uniform, and is what is immediately obvious at every moment to the spectator. But on the other hand, Scipio is a civilian. The comic effect is achieved by letting this military personage, this brilliant uniform, be cast in an utterly incongruous light, incidentally by the fact that the man is half drunk, chiefly by the fact that he is more properly a justice of the peace or the like. So the contradiction is in full swing. At every moment the civilian's mannerisms make the military officer's uniform ridiculous, or the civilian makes the soldier ridiculous. His way of walking and standing, his gestures, etc., will perhaps be ridiculous in and of themselves, but what is more deeply comic is just that they are also more in place and less ridiculous in so far as they belong to the civilian. He is in a military uniform, but has all the civilian businessman's busyness, his mannerisms, the civilian lurch of his whole body, the manner in which he tries to be charming and dangerous where the fair sex is concerned.

This is the essentially comic in Captain Scipio, and what has been set forth here in general terms will provide the basis for what follows.

(1) *Captain Scipio Standing Still*

Captain Scipio is a thick, corpulent man. He does not merely have a tolerable spread, but is, especially for a military man, intolerably paunchy. As regards a military man, not to speak of one in a brilliant uniform, every incongruity instantly produces a comic effect. If a man is tall and powerful, that is as it should be. If he is stout, it will pass. If he is fat, oh well, up to a certain point that will still pass. But go beyond that certain point and it becomes something unmilitary, comic for a military man. Such a figure can at most be tolerated in a major of the militia, just because he is not a military man in the stricter sense. And Captain Scipio's stoutness, especially the protrusion of his belly, not only goes beyond this certain point, but makes him far too big for his breeches. Prince Henry asks Falstaff, who is actually a good deal more rotund, how long it has been since he saw his own knee, to which Falstaff gives the well-known reply, 'My own knee! when I was about thy years, Hal, I was not an eagle's talon in the waist; I could have crept into any alderman's thumb-ring. A plague of sighing and grief! it blows a man up like a bladder.'[7] Now whether it is also sighing and grief that have blown Captain Scipio up, I cannot tell; but blown up he certainly is, and his own knee he certainly cannot see. He stands before us. What a military man! The comic has already registered a *nota bene* with his figure, but now, how does he stand? If one should call the erect military posture standing at attention, then Scipio stands at inattention. The upper part of his body is half stooped over, so that his bandy legs are drawn in under the protruding belly. His whole form thereby resembles a bow. He is complaisant, ingratiating, stooped over – take away the uniform and he completely resembles a countrified civil servant. He takes his shako off to wipe off the sweat. Now, it can also happen that a military man becomes sweaty. But where Scipio is concerned, one gets the impression that he would be soaked in sweat from walking an eighth of a mile, and his brow-mopping completely gives him the character of a civil assessor. It is charming the way he follows his brow-mopping with a gesture that uses the hand as a comb, carefully smoothing down the hair on his half-bald pate.

Can this be a military man? Oh, yes, indeed. Why he is a captain, in brilliant uniform! But everything else is civilian, his whole personality, the marks of the enormously diverse functions of his position as a civil servant, his perpetual half-giddiness: all this constantly renders it impossible for him in any way to express the military; his whole posture, far from approaching it, is a retreat from it.

In this condition he converses with the 'charming landlady'[8] who is to provide him with quarters. The proper approach is again to maintain the duality: the civilian – the military man, with a dash of spirits besides, in which the two are united.[9] Captain S. is charm and gallantry itself; but he is himself a civilian-military amphibian. A uniform, a brilliant uniform and the feminine are essentially related to one another; that is, the feminine in juxtaposition with the brilliant uniform constitutes a demand, which requires something quite definite with respect to posture, etc. If a military man has forgotten that he is in uniform, being brought into the presence of a damsel will immediately remind him of what the uniform requires of him. And Captain Scipio is of course a military man. He performs as well as he can, but not exactly with distinction. A courtly flirtation, the whole body striking an ingratiating attitude, hands fluttering about and ruffling the hair, circling about the 'charming lady' with a graceful hop, etc., all this can be ridiculous enough in and of itself. But it becomes doubly so if, while adorned in the brilliant uniform, the courtier's figure makes a mockery of the most elementary military command: stomach in and chest out.

(2) *Captain Scipio in Motion*

At any rate, at his first entrance Scipio marches in with his detachment. It is necessary that the actor correctly apprehend and express the duality, the ridiculous ambiguity of military and civilian. How shall he come on the stage? Military style requires him to arrive at the head of his troops, or marching along beside them. But, no, Phister understands his art better than that. First, the soldiers come in and place themselves in a row – then comes Captain S. This produces the strong impression that he is lagging behind, however much he hustles. Such an effect is always comical, considering that he is a military man, but this is not all. As the physiologists teach us, the human walk is a perpetual falling. One sees this with unusual clarity in the case of Captain Scipio. With the busyness of a civilian justice of the peace, he comes lagging behind, not walking but not quite falling either. The upper part of his body is tilted over a little and to one side, so that he walks, as we say, a little to the left of his own rump, the one leg falling a few inches short of being drawn in under him. With this infinitely busy, half-hopping sidewise gait, he comes hustling in – lagging behind. An incomparable way of indicating civilian busyness: to arrive in the greatest haste, late! Now he passes the line. It is well known that nature has been so gallant with human beings as to exempt them from having a tail. Yet we also know from the physiologists that at the last joint of the spine there is a faint suggestion of a tail. When Captain Scipio makes his appearance one cannot help imagining a tail on this figure, since he so perfectly suggests a retired English parade-horse now put out for hire, who rouses himself to a little trot.

In this completely civilian, bobtailed business-trot, he passes the line. At this point Phister has hit upon a happy inspiration, playful but in addition contributing essentially to the total comic effect of his role, which is to create discord between the military and the civilian. He lets Captain S. make a silly attempt to establish that he really is a military man by passing the line with sabre drawn — to see that the rank is straight. Splendid! An honest to goodness drillmaster with a little shot of perpetual befuddlement already produces an incomparably comic effect; for someone who is himself befuddled is obviously least of all qualified to direct others, and his striving to do so will have even more unfortunate results than the attempt of someone in bygone times to teach a soldier to stand up straight by letting him lie down crooked. As we have said, such a drillmaster produces a comic effect; but here the civilian in Captain Scipio makes the effect utterly mad.

The more one watches Captain S. the more he evaporates into the void; that is, his comic vacuity becomes more and more obvious.

(3) *God only knows whether Captain Scipio does not Actually Tipple!*

As every aesthetician knows, it is in a certain sense the easiest thing imaginable to portray a man who is drunk; every actor is therefore capable of doing it to a certain extent. For to be drunk is an incommensurability; there is no definitely prescribed stance, gesture, etc., which alone can accurately express it. The most haphazard approach is possible. And at the same time, it is very difficult for the aesthetician to establish norms for an actor where the portrayal of a drunk is

concerned, just because any whim is permitted here. Therefore, while it is a great rarity in any theatre to find an actor
portraying a particular character who can come on the stage
and bow in character – a task which one could properly use as
the test of a would-be actor – on the other hand almost anyone, as we have remarked, can play a drunk, because the role
is so infinitely at random and indefinable.

But Captain S. is not a drunk. He is the sort of man who
from the earliest morning hour and through every moment of
the day, and even if he were roused in the middle of the
night, is always just a bit under the weather, but absolutely
nothing more. He can attend to his business, at least as well as
he could attend to it anyway. He does not get himself drunk,
not even once when the opportunity is offered. One might
rather say that it is an impossibility for him to get drunk;
that just as the virtuous approach a maximum at which it is
said they cannot sin, so Captain S. has approached the maximum at which he cannot get drunk. But on the other hand
there is always the tiniest suggestion of a stagger about him.
This cannot be detected immediately, however, at first glance,
and therefore one really can never be quite certain that he is in
any such condition. Furthermore, Captain S., who through
many years' experience does know with certainty what others
can at best only suspect, is also on his guard to preserve his
dignity and decorum, his complaisant and agreeable manner.
One may assume that the captain (who in his own mind is a
man of the world, a man who has devilishly good form, com-
portment, and refinement in the art of concealment) is fully
possessed by the fancy that he has succeeded extraordinarily
well in concealing it – while it is just this care he takes to
conceal that gives him away.

It is obvious that the problem of conveying all this is altogether more difficult than playing a drunk, and requires a
comedian of such finesse that he would be a rarity in any
theatre. The immediate is in a certain sense negated; it must

never be directly seen that he is drunk, for he is not drunk in that way. The task therefore contains a contradiction: to present (and this again is a contradiction, since to 'present' implies something outward) a man who is drunk – and yet is not drunk, a man who is a little bit befuddled, but still knows enough to take pains, both as a civilian and as a soldier, to conceal it. The comic subtlety consists in making it apparent *telegraphically*, betraying the secret surreptitiously, just through the means by which the captain conceals the true situation.

Herr Phister, now, solves this problem brilliantly. In fact, it is precisely a problem for Herr Phister, that is, a problem of reflection. It is out of the question that one should directly see at some moment that the captain is drunk. But one does entertain a suspicion: God only knows whether Captain Scipio does not actually tipple! It would surely require a comedian of considerable stature just to conceive such a problem correctly, not to speak of solving it; a tipsiness so perfectly kept secret that the clue, the betrayal, is just his attempt to conceal it.

So Captain S. is not drunk, far from it. On the other hand he seems to suffer from a certain flusteration, with the blood rising to his head, accompanied by a slight cough or raspiness. Now, it could be that the weather is warm, or the captain has happened to overexert himself or something of the sort; but no, it cannot be explained in that way. This flusteration seems to attend him constantly, to be something chronic; wherever one meets him and in whatever situation, one will find him flustered. But Captain S., the only one who knows the true situation, is also the man who always knows how to cover up. Hence the continual movement of the hand up to his head, a fluttering of the hand, without anyone being able to conceive exactly why, unless it is to flutter away a certain fog which he fears is gathering around his head. Hence the need to take the shako off so often and gallantly tousle his hair, in order to keep the atmosphere continually in motion around his head, especially when someone comes near him. He does all this so that no one should guess the true reason for his doing it, but that everyone will be led on a false scent, led to suppose that the captain – every time one sees him – has just come from a very long hike, from a burdensome duty or the like, or that he is a great *petit-maître*.[10]

So Captain S. is by no means a drunk; and he, the only one who knows what his condition really is, also knows how to prevent anyone from suspecting the true situation. To be on the safe side, therefore, he brings his hand up to his mouth every so often. One does not see at once what this motion signifies, and besides the captain takes it upon himself to give it the various interpretations which will cover up the true one. If it is a man with whom he is talking, the motion is not to the mouth but from the mouth, an affable gesticulation; if it is a woman, the gesture is transformed so that he is throwing a complaisant kiss with three fingers – and yet the truth is that the motion with his hand is to the mouth or in front of the mouth, using the combined surface of the fingers as a valve to hide and suppress a gentle belch, which would not exactly betray that the captain is drunk, since he is not, but still could easily betray too much, or that the captain has had too much.

So Captain S. is not drunk, by no means; he does not even stagger, much less fall down, far from it. And the captain, the only one who knows what his condition really is, is also the man who knows perfectly well how to conceal it – in such a way that just from his posture one derives, not straight out but indirectly, a suspicion about him. One says of a drunken man that his eyes protrude rigidly out of his head; this is not the case with Captain S. But on the other hand there is in his posture a certain rigidity which is certainly suspicious. For the drunken man reels and lurches; but the posture of the respectable man, who quite secretly feels a bit unsteady on his feet, has just this suspicious rigidity. The captain's gait is a contradiction. He pulls, so to speak, himself and his body together, arms arched almost like a dancing cavalier's; he puts – his best foot forward. But he get no farther, he cannot entirely bring off this ceremonious appearance, cannot entirely assume the poise for which he is striving. As we have said, he puts his best foot forward, but, when he is about to put the other in front of it, in that instant – for now he has taken the step – the total impression is of a certain wobbliness. But then it begins all over again, he again puts his best foot forward. In the instant when he stands, with arms bent, in a complaisant bow, on the best foot – yes, it is superbly done, it is splendidly concealed that he has had a little too much. But still, still it is quite impossible to remain standing in this position, and in the next instant a suspicion arises, which never quite becomes more than a suspicion, since now he has again assumed the position on his best foot. A suspicion arises: God only knows whether Captain S. does not actually tipple!

So Captain S. is by no means drunk. And on the contrary he is a military man in a brilliant uniform; he is further a civil servant, in the police force; he is finally, in a certain crude sense, a man of the world, he is adroit, he knows how to conceal his true state of affairs. To portray such a figure is a task for a subtle comedian. One can say in advance: that is a role for Phister. And when one has seen it, one is fully convinced: it is a role for Phister.

(4) *In the Second Act of the Play Captain Scipio is Accidentally Sober*

Captain Scipio is accidentally sober in the second act of the play. It must be noted that this is accidental; for if it had any essentially deeper significance, if, for example, he had decided to give up drinking on moral grounds, the comic effect would be sacrificed. The situation is this. In spite of all his efforts Captain Scipio has not succeeded in apprehending the criminal whom he has been sent to arrest. In his zeal he makes a vow not to taste wine or liquor until he has succeeded in arresting the culprit.[11] One has all the more sympathy with his pathetic lines when he has to conduct a house inspection on a hermit who happens to drink wine instead of water. He cries out, 'What torment, when I myself have vowed not to drink anything but water, to have to make a call on a hermit who has vowed not to drink anything but wine.'[12]

Just because Phister has so splendidly portrayed Scipio in the first act, he has therefore also correctly seen that there is no essential difference at all between Scipio's appearance in the first act and his appearance in the second. That may seem odd, but it is quite true: a man can be foggy because of having too much to drink; but a man can be almost in the same condition just because he has had nothing to drink. When a man who has been addicted to the constant use of intoxicating drink, even without really being drunk, suddenly leaves off drinking, then he is for some time in essentially the same condition, because he has gone slack, in fact he is apparently almost more intoxicated than he was when he drank. Just by imbibing the customary quantity of spirits, such a man almost comes to seem completely sober; and when one day he is completely sober he seems much rather to be almost drunk.

The difference in Captain Scipio between the first and the second act is therefore only this, that in the second act he has a little less of that forced tension, that instead his figure is suffused with a certain melancholy languor, a kind of *tristitia*.[13] Now for the first time he looks more like a drunken man; his gait is unsure and meandering, his arms hang down loosely, his eyes stare, he reels, his legs will not quite carry him, he no longer has a best foot with which to strive in the least for poise – and why? Because he is now sober.

Again, Phister has understood this correctly, that what is witty in the role consists in this: in the first act to conceal and only quite indirectly let it be detected that Scipio is a little bit drunk; in the second act to let him almost appear to be a drunk – because he is sober.

———————————

This brief article is a recollection. It has been many years since its author saw *Ludovic,* and it has already been some years since the piece was performed at all. I cannot resist making a comment in that connection. The usual theatre critics attend on the first evening that a new play is presented; and merely seeing it that one time is all they need in order to pass judgement on the play and every single actor – a Phister, a Rosenkilde, a Nielsen, a Wiehe, a Fru Heiberg, a Madame Nielsen – who has sometimes brought many months and all his genius, his thoughtfulness, his diligence to the interpretation of his role.

It is otherwise with this brief article. It has gained no advantage over Herr Phister, but has only striven faithfully to reproduce what he has already produced, what is therefore his. But it has to a high degree the character of discretion – and surely Herr Phister could also lay claim to discretion, and will hence know how to value it. That is why it has been written. Its author is essentially occupied with quite other tasks than those of theatre critic, which are none of his concern. But in such a small country as Denmark it is a duty for anyone who may be able to perform it, and as such is not a matter of indifference to him after all, to employ his scanty moments of leisure, enjoyably and restfully, if possible, in paying back a little of the debt we owe our great artists of the stage, a debt that only continues to grow with every attempt of the ordinary newspaper critic to pay it back.

December, 1848

Procul

NOTES

[1] (p. 65) title page – This ponderous title is probably intended as a reminder that the case of the particular actress discussed in the essay is an example of a general category. Her metamorphosis (*a* crisis) simply illustrates one form of *the* crisis through which any actress must pass on the way to mature artistry. In Kierkegaard's manuscript the title stood originally as 'The Crisis in the Life of an Actress', but the additional clause was later inserted.

The pseudonym *'Inter et Inter'* ('Between and Between') suggests the intermission at the theatre, but doubtless is also intended to reflect the fact that the article is only an interlude between the religious works which now comprise Kierkegaard's main task. Inscribed in the manuscript and later deleted is the entry: 'From a Dead Man's Papers'. The Danish text can be found in Vol. XIV of the new edition of Kierkegaard's *Samlede Vaerker* (Gyldendal, 1963).

[2] (p. 67) 'fund *ad usus publicos*' – a public fund established for the support of deserving persons.

[3] (p. 68) 'this burdensome splendour' – In her memoirs Fru Heiberg often testifies just how burdensome this splendour was to her. The public's favour became 'a kind of idolization that often alarmed me. Applause on the stage, as well as poems and flowers which were sent to my home (at that time people had not yet taken up the outlandish custom, which I have never found attractive or proper, of throwing flowers up on the stage . . .), and gifts and half-crazy love letters besides, were the order of the day. When I showed myself in the streets

people followed in order to catch a glimpse of me. The high
and the low sought by every means to come into contact with
me. People imitated me, not only in the theatre but in life.
Whatever the cut of my clothing or my hair, theirs must be
the same, and a swarm of women made themselves ridiculous
by copying me in everything without discrimination.' *Et Liv*,
I, pp. 160–61. Fortunately for Fru Heiberg, journalistic photo-
graphy had not yet come into its own.

[4] (p. 73) 'Caesar – and his luck' – According to Plutarch,
Caesar 38, Caesar said this to the captain of his ship when the
ship was in distress during a voyage to Brundisium (Brindisi).

[5] (p. 73) 'at her beck and call' – literally, 'the luck even stands
on a stick for her', i.e. performs stunts for her, is at her disposal.

[6] (p. 74) 'put on display . . . and to that extent cannot properly
be called an actress at all' – an untranslatable play on the
Danish word for 'actress': *Skuespillerinde* (lit. show-player).
On account of such things as her beauty, she is presented as a
Skue (show) all right, and to that extent cannot properly be
called a Skue*spillerinde*.

[7] (p. 74) 'the restlessness of infinity' – In the Hegelian philosophy the true infinite is qualitative, the realization or self-
reflection of the idea, finally in an existing life or consciousness.
This is contrasted with the 'bad infinite' which is, among other
things, the mere endless proliferation of finite forms, 'finitude
run riot'; it is also contrasted with the abstract and unchanging
universality of a purely ideal form. The true infinite is, according to Hegel, 'the ultimate nature of life, the soul of the world,
the universal life-blood, which courses everywhere, and whose
flow is neither disturbed nor checked by any obstructing
distinction, but is itself every distinction that arises, as well as

that into which distinctions are dissolved; pulsating within itself, but ever motionless, shaken to its depths, but still at rest' (*The Phenomenology of Mind*, tr. by Baillie [London, Allen and Unwin and New York, The Macmillan Company, Revised Edition, 1949], p. 208).

[8] (p. 75) 'you see Rosenkilde' – C. N. Rosenkilde, the Danish actor and a personal friend of Kierkegaard's. Croxall quotes from the *Memoirs* of the actress, Julie Sødring, Rosenkilde's daughter, an account of how Kierkegaard and her father used to perform 'psychological experiments' on other people, e.g. observing the reaction of a poor woman when they gave her a five dollar bill. (*Kierkegaard Commentary*, Nisbet, 1956, p. 110.) During the same year in which *The Crisis* was written, Kierkegaard prepared an outline-sketch towards an article on 'Rosenkilde as "Hammer"' (in Heiberg's vaudeville *The Inseparables*), subtitled 'An Attempt at Recollection by One Who is Grateful'. But no finished article ever resulted from the attempt.

[9] (p. 77) 'She relates herself expressively' – literally, 'she relates herself in soulfulness' *(Sjaelfuldhed)*.

[10] (p. 77) 'Let me see you copy that' – literally 'can you copy me that' or 'can you imitate that'. *(kan Du gjøre mig det efter.)* A paraphrase might be, 'Here is the original you were trying to copy.'

Fru Heiberg reports an interesting conversation with Grundtvig, the famous Danish reformer, preacher, educator, and hymn-writer, which illustrates the point. Grundtvig, now an aged man and apparently rather out of humour on this occasion, had remarked that he scarcely ever attended the theatre, because when an actor played the same role over and over his performance must become 'nothing but pure affectation'. Fru Heiberg replied that in this case a preacher who preached the same sermon more than once must also be indulging in affectation. 'This remark of mine apparently did not please him; he answered, hardly being able to repress his anger, since his lips trembled: "No, I beg your pardon! A parson can preach the same sermon twice, because the words are his own." – "But a good actor appropriates his poet's words as though they were his own," I answered, and I tried to make my point clear to him, explaining how wonderfully an actor is able to wed himself to the poetic work which he is rendering . . . [Grundtvig] would have been amazed if he could have seen what was happening within me during my rehearsal of Shakespeare's Juliet! No, truly, my joy and ecstasy in it were no affectation.' Fru Heiberg also suggests that the actor is able to feel what the poet himself has felt in conceiving his work, and may even feel it more powerfully than the poet himself. (*Et Liv*, I, pp. 418–19).

[11] (p. 78) This paragraph was one which particularly pleased Fru Heiberg. After expressing her great pleasure at *The Crisis* in general, especially at Kierkegaard's sympathetic understanding of the obstacles an actress must overcome in her relation to the public, she especially praises this paragraph: 'It is a wonderful surprise for a practicing artist to read what an inspired theorist is able to express clearly and distinctly about things which the artist has *felt* in the highest degree without being capable himself of finding the words to express and elucidate his feelings. Thus I have always been astonished at what Kierkegaard says on p. 162 of the same article.' Fru Heiberg then quotes the paragraph in full. 'These remarks coming from a non-actor,' she adds, 'were what astounded me. They are absolutely right; I have many times felt exactly as is here described. In the wings all the weight of anxiety, in the play or at rehearsals light as a bird. Those who are not and ought not to be actors have just the opposite experience. Off-stage and in the wings, confident. What is there to be anxious about? they say. But as soon as they go on the stage

anxiety overcomes them like a nightmare. It is therefore a fact that young dilettantes are rarely anxious the first time they appear. But year by year anxiety grows stronger as the burden of their art is laid more heavily upon them. How little the public is aware of all this is best seen by the way it is always touched and tender towards anyone who shows his anxiety on the stage before them. But the public does not realize that this visible anxiety is the surest sign that one is unable to lose himself so completely in the play that he becomes another person and is no longer himself as he is in private life' (*Et Liv*, I, pp. 425–26). Croxall quotes this passage in *Kierkegaard Commentary* (Welwyn, James Nisbet & Co., 1956), pp. 113–14. I have revised his translation.

[12] (p. 79) 'the daughter of the regiment' – in Donizetti's opera of that name.

[13] (p. 81) 'Just for that reason, all those who in truth . . ." – Many of these reflection in Part III have at least as much to do with Kierkegaard's own case as with Fru Heiberg's. This paragraph is an obvious example. Kierkegaard was always disdainful of the tactic here described, of concealing oneself from the public except on special occasions in order to surround one's person and works with an aura of mysterious grandeur. He himself followed the practice of the 'unselfish servants of the truth' here described, walking daily in the market-place and chatting with everyone who would talk. The results were as he says, that his works were depreciated in the popular mind because of this familiarity. Furthermore, he became especially vulnerable to the vulgar attack of *The Corsair* because of this habit of his; *The Corsair* caricatured his figure as it appeared in these walks, commenting on such things as the length of his trousers. Finally, as a result of this attack, people openly made fun of him in the streets; children are said to have followed him hooting 'either/or, either/or' at him; it hurt him deeply at last

to have to give up his walks because of this petty persecution, and thus to lose a contact with 'the common man' which he seems to have enjoyed. See *The Point of View*, Chapter II, A, pp. 45 ff., which directly parallels this paragraph.

[14] (p. 81) 'Henry IV's address to Prince Henry' – in *Henry IV*, Part I, Act III, Scene 2.

[15] (p. 82) '"*mundus vult decipi*" . . . "*decipiatur ergo*"' – 'the world wishes to be deceived' . . . 'therefore let it be deceived'.

[16] (p. 82) 'Suppose that an author . . .' – Again, in the first part of this paragraph, Kieregaard clearly has his own case in mind. He was the 'highly productive author' who by unsparing exertions poured out books at a rate hardly rivalled by any other major thinker. He created practically his whole vast corpus within the space of ten years. The consequence, of which he often complains bitterly in the *Journals*, was that he was generally accused of carelessness. Furthermore, the author whom he seems to have had particularly in mind in the little caricature about the producer at great intervals of decorative little copybooks was none other than Heiberg. See the following paragraph from *The Journals*, also written during 1847:

'Quite right. My *Edifying Discourses in Various Moods* are liked, particularly the last one, and why? Because they are short and because the whole thing, by comparison with what I have produced, is small. That is the whole point: twopenny literature. The big book on Adler I have kept back, and so with the help of a deception people have become profound critics – they only see a small book, *ergo* I have spent a lot of time on it, *ergo* it is written with exceptional care. Alas, I suppose I must conceal what I can do. If I let my true wing-spread be seen again then all the gossip about my working quickly and carelessly will begin again. Miserable provincial

town! And Heiberg and his type take part in that gossip –
because he himself is only a twopenny author, and so has to
maintain that so great an achievement is done carelessly,
particularly when the time is so short' (Dru translation, 675).

[17] (p. 82) 'the late Chaplain to the Court in Berlin, the otherwise so highly-gifted Theremin' – Dr. Franz Theremin,
1780–1846, the Head-Chaplain-to-the-Court *(Oberhofprediger)*
since 1814 and a member of the Supreme Consistorial Council
(Oberconsistorialrath) since 1834. During his later years he had
to restrict his preaching activities because of illness. Kierkegaard's countryman, Martensen, the Hegelian theologian and
later bishop, had been made Chaplain to the Danish Court in
1845. In view of Kierkegaard's continuing implacable opposi-
ion to Martensen, the fact of Martensen's holding this office
probably prompted Kierkegaard's rather irreverent treatment
of the office here.

[18] (p. 83) 'to secure the Right Reverend Head-Chaplain's
going out and coming in.' – See *Psalm* 121: 8, 'The Lord shall
preserve thy going out and thy coming in from this time forth,
and even for evermore.'
At the time that *The Crisis* was published, Bishop Mynster's
age and health apparently permitted him to preach no more
than every fourth Sunday. However, as Kierkegaard noted in
his *Journals* at that time, doubtless with the present paragraph
in mind, the church was not overflowing when he did preach.
Kierkegaard thought there was cause to praise God in this
fact, since 'one can see that no deception has come to his aid.
On the contrary, he has now working against him the deception
that he is an old man, and therefore he can never do any harm
by the fact of only preaching every fourth Sunday.' But he
adds, in a passage that points towards his later 'attack upon
Christendom', that there are deceptions enough in Christendom, for example in treating the priesthood as a way of earning

a living, and in mistaking ecclesiastical pomp and glitter for the fear of God (*Papirer*, IX, 188 [not included in Dru's translation]).

[19] (p. 83) '"*Sanguis martyrum est semen ecclesiae*"' – 'The blood of the martyrs is the seed of the church' (Tertullian, *Apologeticus* 50).

[20] (p. 84) 'the children in the market-place' – See *Matthew* 11: 16–19.

[21] (p. 84) '*spiritus asper*' – a grammatical term, the rough or aspirated breathing in the pronunciation of Greek vowels when they appear at the beginning of some words, transliterated with an 'h'. In Kierkegaard's rather fanciful image here, this rough breathing is being contrasted with the 'smooth breathing' – without aspiration – of the later, habitual admiration.

[22] (p. 85) 'the Promethean and the Epimethean' – The two brothers, Prometheus and Epimetheus, traditionally represented foresight and hindsight; their names mean 'forethought' and 'afterthought'. The 'naturalists' whom Kierkegaard had in mind were probably of Schelling's school.

[23] (p. 86) 'time is the dialectical that comes from without' – In the Hegelian philosophy time is dialectical in that every particular existing thing and every particular state of affairs is destroyed by the passing of time, but in such a way that what is essential, universal, substantial and true in the transitory moment is preserved. But the idea, which is the essential, universal, etc., itself is still more profoundly dialectical, since it transcends all particularity and even time itself. Thus, says Hegel, Cronos devours all his children, but 'Zeus, who gave birth to Athene out of his head and whose circle included

Apollo and the Muses, conquered Time and set a limit to its lapse'. Again, 'Time is the negative element in the sensuous world. Thought is the same negativity, but its deepest, its infinite form' (Hegel, *Reason in History*, tr. with an Introduction by Robert S. Hartman [New York, The Liberal Arts Press, 1953], pp. 91–93). By her relation to idea, our actress is armed with a dialectic which is master over time; time simply serves to bring her potential embodiment of the idea to actual fruition.

[24] (p. 86) *'erectioris ingenii'* – or more elevated temperament.

[25] (p. 88) *'quod desideratur'* – what is desired.

[26] (p. 90) 'a certain ethicist' – Judge William, the 'married man' who is the pseudonymous author of *Eithor/Or* Volume II and of the essay 'Various Observations about Marriage in Reply to Objections' in *Stages on Life's Way*. In the latter, the judge, who is Kierkegaard's spokesman for the ethical stance in life, devotes a long and very difficult footnote to the praise of Madame Nielsen, the other great lady of the Danish stage at that time. In opposition to the 'aesthetic' view that only the beauty of a woman's early youth is perfect, the judge is defending the thesis that a woman grows in beauty with the years, and points to Madame Nielsen as a vindication of the point. Not that Madame Nielsen fulfils an ethical ideal in a sense simply opposed to the aesthetic. The judge always argues that the aesthetic is fulfilled, not on its own terms as such, but in the ethical relationship; e.g. the aesthetic beauty of young love is perfected in the ethical relationship of marriage. A woman cannot of course retain the bloom of youth, but then the essential beauty of woman is not fully expressed during this or any other single period of her life, but unfolds itself in her total development through all periods of life and their diverse situations. This is the genius which Madame

Nielsen seems to the judge to express in her art. 'The actress who in our theatre really represents the feminine, without being restricted to one side of it, without being either propped up or brought to grief by some accidental feature of it, without being limited to some fragmentary period of its course, is Madame Nielsen . . . her total presentation is united in what one may call the essential feminine. Many actresses become great and are admired for their virtuosity in relation to one side of the feminine; but this admiration, which is indeed given proper expression in all manner of momentary rejoicing, is from its beginning the prey of time, when the contingencies vanish on which the triumphal presentation depends. Since Madame Nielsen's potency is the essential feminine, her range embraces the essential even in less significant roles, provided the play offers her an essential situation (as a lady-love in vaudeville, as a mother in an idyl, etc.): embraces the essential in the noble figures, and also the essential in the depraved. . . . But just as regards her range, so also is her achievement an essential one, not the shortlived triumph of a moment but such that time has no power over her. In every period of her life, she will undertake the new assignments and will express the essential, just as she has done from the beginning of her brilliant career.' The judge ventures to predict that when she is sixty she will portray the grandmother with the same perfection with which she earlier endowed the role of the young girl, always in virtue of the essential feminine; not through special techniques or spectacular impressions, 'but with the dedication which is the pact of pure femininity with the imperishable. Whereas one can otherwise easily be led in the theatre to reflect on the vanity of life and youth and beauty and enchantment, one feels serene in admiring her, because one knows that this will not perish.' (For the full text of this long footnote, see *Stages on Life's Way*, tr. Water Lowrie [Princeton University Press, and Oxford University Press 1940], pp. 133–34. I have considerably revised Lowrie's translation in this excerpt.)

[27] (p. 90) 'Eureka' – 'I have found it!' as Archimedes is supposed to have cried in the streets of Syracuse after disdovering a method of determining the purity of gold.

[28] (p. 91) 'Summer 1847' – In the original manuscript Kierkegaard added, then crossed out, the comment that 'the article is in fact still older, but I do not remember exactly'.

[1] (p. 93) title page – 'A.' – This pseudonym, if an initial can count as a pseudonym, doubtless refers to the first volume of *Either/Or*, which Victor Eremita, the pseudonymous editor of the whole work, designates for convenience' sake as 'the papers of A.' Certainly the piece constitutes a kind of addendum to the great essay on Mozart's *Don Juan* which is included in that volume under the title 'The Immediate Stages of the Erotic or the Musical Erotic'. The adoption of Victor's cataloguing mark as a pseudonym was probably an after-thought, since the references in the piece to the essay in *Either/Or* generally seem to imply that the latter is the work of another author. The Danish text can be found in Vol. xviii of the new edition of Kierkegaard's *Samlede Vaerker* (Gyldendal, 1964).

[2] (p. 95) 'Mozart's *Don Juan*' *(Don Giovanni)* – After not having been performed on the Danish stage since November 1840, the opera was given five performances between February and May 1845.

[3] (p. 95) 'Socrates had a fine old rule . . .' – Kierkegaard seems to have had in mind a passage in Diogenes Laertius ii: 22. Socrates is said to have remarked of the writings of Heraclitus that since what he could understand of it was good he was inclined to give the philosoper the benefit of the doubt regarding those things which he was not able to understand.

[4] (p. 95) 'Herr Hansen's performance' – J. Chr. Hansen (1812–80) sang the title role in Mozart's opera from 1839 to 1870.

[5] (p. 96) 'the duet with Zerlina . . .' – Act I, Scene 7 in the Schirmer edition of the opera, preceded by recitatives in Scene 6.

[6] (p. 96) 'the first scene with Anna' – Act I, Scene 1.

[7] (p. 97n) 'What he said in the old days to Elvira . . .' – Act I, Scene 3, shortly before Leporello's famous List Aria in Scene 4. Kierkegaard is following a Danish translation by L. Kruse (Copenhagen, 1807). Cf. *Either/Or*, I (Doubleday Anchor edition, p. 131), where this line of Leporello's is cited as an example of Juan's distinctively musical presence in the opera. He is always present in the music of the opera, even when he is off-stage. It is Juan's virtuosity that he is no sooner present than he vanishes, yet even when he has vanished the 'force of nature' which is Juan lingers on, e.g. in the music of Leporello's List Aria itself.

[8] (p. 98) 'Madam Kragh' – Boline Margrethe Kragh, *née* Abrahamsen (1810–39), who played Zerlina from 1829–39.

[9] (p. 98n) 'the profound and Greek touch . . .' – Kierkegaard has in mind the Greek conception of Nemesis, the doom which the higher powers inflict on the hero by means that often seem trivial in themselves.

[10] (p. 98) *'au niveau'* – at a level, on the same plane.

[11] (p. 98) *'batti, batti'* – Act I, Scene 12.

[12] (p. 99) 'Anna . . . rages for revenge' – Act I, Scene 10.

[13] (p. 100) '. . . finds Leporello to be just as guilty . . .' – Act II, Scenes 17–21.

[14] (p. 100) *'ausser sich'* – beside herself.

[15] (p. 100) '. . . deeply tragic situation in the second act' –
Scene 15.

[16] (p. 100) '. . . an author has said that it is almost gruesome' –
Either/Or, I, p. 131. Instead of 'gruesome' Swenson translates
'grusom' as 'cruel', but to say that 'the mockery which is sometimes made of Elvira's love is almost cruel' is an impossible
understatement.

[17] (p. 100) 'Elvira . . . conveys her whole pathos to Zerlina' –
Act I, Scene 8.

[18] (p. 101) 'Now for Don Juan. . . .' – Since the point of this
paragraph is rather obscure, yet is quite crucial in understanding what follows, a little commentary may be in order. An
important key to the argument in Part II of the article is a
point already argued in *Either/Or*, I (e.g. see pp. 96–102): Don
Juan is pure sensuousness, too direct, uncalculating, immediate
in his sexuality to be a seducer in the strict sense. This is why,
in Kierkegaard's view, he is 'absolutely musical'; he is the
supreme operatic subject, and opera is the only appropriate
medium in which to represent him, for music is the art form
of immediacy. Don Juan is most fully in his own element in
the act of conquest, and therefore at this point above all there
is no place for the sort of artful device described in our paragraph. Real seduction, on the other hand, is a crafty art, un-
suitable to opera. The 'seducer' *par excellence*, Johannes of the
'Diary' in *Either/Or*, I, is both calculating and imaginative to
a pathological degree. Were it his good fortune to be a singer,
he might have brought off such a manœuvre as that described
in the paragraph. But not Don Juan. A seducer is a figure of
literature or drama, Juan of opera.

[19] (p. 101) *'omnibus numeris absoluta'* – perfect in every respect.

[20] (p. 102) '"a golden apple in a silver bowl"' – *Proverbs* 25:11, where 'a word fitly spoken' is so described.

[21] (p. 102) 'Don Juan is no . . . seducer . . .' – 'To be a seducer requires a certain amount of reflection and consciousness, and as soon as this is present, then it is proper to speak of cunning and intrigues and crafty plans. This consciousness is lacking in Don Juan. Therefore he does not seduce. He desires, and this desire acts seductively. To that extent he seduces.' (*Either/Or*, I, p. 97; see p. 99, and note 18 above.)

[22] (p. 102) 'the guitar-aria' – Act II, Scene 16.

[23] (p. 102) 'Don Juan joins in (*"poverina, poverina"*) with Elvira's opening aria' – Act I, Scene 32. To Don Juan's line *'poverina, poverina'* – 'the poor girl' – the Schirmer edition assigns the stage note, 'with contemptuous pity'; but Kierkegaard insists below that it is to be sung 'straight', without irony.

[24] (p. 102) '. . . an author has pointed out' – *Either/Or*, I, pp. 119–22.

[25] (p. 103) '. . . he tells Elvira . . . "that was only a little diversion!"' – Act I, Scene 7.

[26] (p. 103) '*κατ' ἐξοχὴν*' – *par excellence*, to the ultimate degree.

[27] (p. 103) '(music being a more universal medium)' – in the sense that it does not express specific meanings or particular individuals as such, but expresses pure sensuousness, a 'force of nature'. See *Either/Or*, I, pp. 65 ff. *et passim*.

[28] (p. 104) 'the serious category' – morality.

[29] (p. 104) 'Zerlina is . . . blown about constantly in the wind' – Kierkegaard appears to be punning here, since 'to be in the wind' is also an idiom implying that one is popular, particularly a girl much in demand, or that one is being fêted. The other sense of being 'in the wind' recalls previous descriptions of Zerlina.

[30] (p. 105) 'I ought to be looking soon for other legs to walk on' – again an apparent pun impossible to preserve. The last clause contains an idiom *(faae andre Ben at gaae paa)* which means, roughly, to be set straight or put in one's place. But the whole final sentence may also be an oblique reference to Kierkegaard's own awkward appearance. Within a few months after the publication of this piece his thin legs and unsteady gait became a recurrent target of *The Corsair*'s caricature and ridicule.

[1] (p. 107) title page – 'Herr Phister as Captain Scipio' was completed in December of 1848, a few months after *The Crisis* was published. Apparently Kierkegaard thought at one time of publishing it in *The Fatherland*, and the carefully revised manuscript appears to have been prepared for publication; but for reasons that probably had nothing to do with the worth of the article he seems never in fact to have submitted it. Perhaps he did give a copy of it to Phister, who was a neighbour of his at the time. There is a note with the manuscript inscribed to 'Herr Phister the Actor' in which he says that the article 'is as though designed for only one reader', Phister himself. The Danish text is available in *Søren Kierkegaards Papirer*, edited by P. A. Heiberg and V. Kuhr (Gyldendalske Boghandel – Nordisk Forlag, Kjøbenhavn og Kristiania, 1920), IX B, pp. 383–407, giving both the final form of the manuscript and portions altered and excised in the revisions.

Ludovic is a comic opera in two acts, the original French text by J. H. Vernoy de Saint-Georges, music by L. J. F. Hérold and J. F. Halévy. The Danish translation, by Th. Overskou, was published by the Royal Theatre in Copenhagen in 1834. It was in the repertoire of the Royal Theatre, with Phister in the role of 'Scipio, Captain in the Papal Police Corps', from 1834 to 1841, and received one more performance in Kierkegaard's lifetime, on 11 June 1846.

Phister was a long-time favourite of Kierkegaard's at the Royal Theatre. In the essay on Scribe's *The First Love* in *Either/Or*, I, he speaks of Phister, Fru Heiberg, Frydendahl, and Stage as the 'four-leaf clover' of the Danish stage (p. 237). Again: 'Behold Phister, you almost become ill when you let your glance rest on the infinitely fresh stupidity that is stamped on his countenance. And yet it is not an immediate dullness; his glance still has an enthusiasm which in its foolishness is reminiscent of the past. No one is born with such a face, it has a history' (p. 277).

Procul, the pseudonym assumed by Kierkegaard for this article, is Latin for 'afar off' or 'at a distance'. This pseudonym seems to have been chosen with the passage which appears on p. 113 in the text in mind, which refers to the 'infinitely distant' relationship between the reflective critic and the reflective artist whom he admires, an admiration 'as aristocratically distant as mind can be from mind.'

[2] (p. 110) 'all infatuation; is really basically self-love' – See *The Works of Love*, Part I, Chapter II A. Especially relevant here is the marginal comment, preserved in the *Papirer*, VIII B, p. 124, which Kierkegaard made on the passage in *The Works of Love*:

At the basis of love lies an impulse, and at the basis of friendship lies a disposition, but impulse and disposition are natural qualities, and natural qualities are always selfish; only the eternal qualities of spirit can drive out selfishness. Therefore in love and friendship there is still a concealed selfishness. When a girl, of the sort the poet rejoices to hear about and celebrate, can only love one single person in all the world, that is certainly real love; but this love is also the most glowing expression of partiality. In partiality, especially when it blazes forth in this form, is concealed precisely self-love, as every girl or lover comes to realize . . . in such partiality there lies a conscious or unconscious wilfulness, which arbitrarily demands to have its own way. To be able to love this one person is the satisfaction of infatuation and partiality, but also basically of self-love. To despair when such love is disappointed shows precisely that this love was self-love. But just because love denies that judgement, it dares express itself in the prodigious claim to love another person more than oneself. Alas! for the infatuated one has still not learned how, in the seriousness and truth of eternity, to love himself [my translation].

³ (p. 110) '. . . in the way Trop "stoddies"' – in J. L. Heiberg's *The Critic and the Beast* (*Recensenten og Dyret* [Kjøbenhavn, 1827], pp. 15 ff. – Scene 3).

⁴ (p. 111) 'Therefore there is perhaps hardly another actor on our stage. . . .' – Kierkegaard was not alone in this high estimate of Phister as a reflective artist. J. L. Heiberg, as a dramatist who worked closely with Phister, also held him in great respect and for similar reasons, according to Fru Heiberg: 'Of all the actors Phister was the one whom Heiberg regarded most highly. He admired his quick and sure perceptiveness, his taste and his painstaking care in interpreting even the most insignificant word, his restraint and his fidelity in the service of the poet.' (*Et Liv gjenoplevet i Erindringen*, I, p. 194.)

⁵ (p. 112) '. . . an exchange like that which Poul Møller has preserved . . .' – See Poul Møller, *Efterladte Skrifter (Posthumous Works)* (Kjøbenhavn, 1843), Vol. III, p. 159. I have taken liberties in translating the exchange, with some debt to Popeye the Sailor.

⁶ (p. 113) '*Gemütlichkeit*' – coziness, comfortable cordiality, good-natured congeniality.

⁷ (p. 117) 'Prince Henry asks Falstaff . . .' – *Henry IV*, Part I, Act II, Scene 4.

⁸ (p. 118) '. . . he converses with the "charming landlady" . . . – *Ludovic*, Act I, Scene 6.

[9] (p. 118) '. . . a dash; of spirits besides, in which the two are united' – This is a little parody on the Hegelian concept of Spirit *(Geist)*, which is the Absolute in which all contradictions are reconciled.

[10] (p. 123) *'Petit-maître'* – dandy, fop.

[11] (p. 125) 'In his zeal he makes a vow . . .' – Act II, Scene 3.

[12] (p. 125) '. . . his pathetic lines when he has to conduct a house inspection on a hermit . . .' – Act II, Scene 15.

[13] (p. 125) *'tristitia'* – sadness, melancholy, moroseness.

INDEX

harper ✦ torchbooks

---

† The New American Nation Series, edited by Henry Steele Commager and Richard B. Morris.
‡ American Perspectives series, edited by Bernard Wishy and William E. Leuchtenburg.
* The Rise of Modern Europe series, edited by William L. Langer.
** History of Europe series, edited by J. H. Plumb.
¶ Researches in the Social, Cultural and Behavioral Sciences, edited by Benjamin Nelson.
§ The Library of Religion and Culture, edited by Benjamin Nelson.
Σ Harper Modern Science Series, edited by James R. Newman.
⁰ Not for sale in Canada.
△ Not for sale in the U. K.

2